A FALKLANDS DIARY

Jean Austin worked as a modern languages teacher in Portugal, Kuwait, Cyprus and Nigeria. It was in Nigeria that she met and married her husband, J. A. Jones, OBE, who was a member of the Colonial Administrative Service. She travelled with him to his various postings in Nigeria, the Gambia, the Solomon Islands, Kiribati and the Falklands Islands. They retired in 1984 and now live in Garlieston, Scotland, in her maternal home.

A FALKLANDS DIARY

Winds of Change in a Distant Colony

JEAN AUSTIN

The Radcliffe Press

LONDON • NEW YORK

Published in 2009 by The Radcliffe Press
6 Salem Road, London W2 4BU

Distributed in the United States and Canada Exclusively by
Palgrave Macmillan
175 Fifth Avenue, New York NY 10010

ISBN 987 1 84511 713 9 (HB)

A full CIP record is available from the Library of Congress

Library of Congress Catalog card: available

Copy-edited and typeset by 4word Ltd, Bristol.
Printed and bound in Great Britain by
CPI Antony Rowe, Chippenham

FSC
Mixed Sources
Product group from well-managed forests and other controlled sources
Cert no. SGS-COC-2953
www.fsc.org
© 1996 Forest Stewardship Council

Contents

Illustrations

Acronyms and Abbreviations

AES	MV *AES*, a Danish cargo vessel
AGB	nickname for A. G. Barton
BAS	British Antarctic Survey
FIDS	Falkland Islands Dependencies Survey
FIGAS	Falkland Islands Government Air Service
GH	Government House
HE	His Excellency
HMS	Her Majesty's Ship
LADE	Argentine Air Force Airline
MV	motor vessel
PWD	Public Works Department
RAF	Royal Air Force
RMS	Royal mail ship
SS	steamship

Glossary

albatross	(Spanish: *albatros*) amphibian aircraft designed for air/sea search and rescue work, operated by the Argentine navy and air force (by the latter on the temporary air service from Comodoro Rivadavia to Stanley established under the Joint Statement of Buenos Aires of 1 July 1971).
Buenos Aires	City of ten million inhabitants, which is approximately half the country's total population. It is the capital of the Republic of Argentina, which has the largest population of British descent of any country outside the Commonwealth.
British delegation	This delegation to the talks with Argentina on communications consisted of members of the Foreign and Commonwealth Office and of the Falkland Islands Legislative Council.
camp	Name used to refer to all the country outside the capital, Stanley: from the Spanish *campo*.
camper	A person who lives in camp.
colony	Crown Colony of the Falkland Islands

	and Dependencies. The dependencies are the islands of South Georgia and South Sandwich.
Colonial Secretary	Head of the colony's civil service who acts as governor in the latter's absence.
Deputy Governor	This is usually the colonial secretary when appointed to administer the government while the governor is away from the seat of government but still in the colony.
FIGAS	The government air service that operates two de Haviland (Canada) 'Beaver' floatplane aircraft.
Government House	The governor's official residence.
HE	His Excellency. Term of address for the governor who, as the queen's representative, is the most senior figure in the colony on all formal occasions. The governmor of the Falklands full title is Governor and Commander-in-Chief of the Falkland Islands and Dependencies and High Commissioner of the British Antarctic Territory.
Joint Statement	The culmination of the second round of talks between Britain and Argentina. It was signed, subject to ratification by the participants, in a special ceremony in Buenos Aires on 1 July 1971, and it provided for the freeing of communications between Argentina and the Falkland Islands. It

	covered most channels of communication – transport, freight, mail, telegraphs, telephones, education and tourism.
kelper	Name by which Falkland Islanders prefer to be known and derived from the heavy concentrations of kelp (particularly *macrocystis pyrifera*) that grow round the colony's coast.
LADE	A developmental airline run as an integral part of the Argentine air force to provide subsidized communication to the republic's economically less advanced areas.
mainland	In this context it refers to the South American mainland.
Malvinas (Las Islas)	Spanish name for the Falkland Islands. It derives from the French *Les Malouines*, in its turn attributable to the early connection with the islands of seafarers from the French port of St Malo.
Monte	Nickname for Montevideo, the capital of the Republic of Uruguay.
smoko	tea break.
Rounds 1, 2 and 3	Serial numbers for talks on communications held since mid-1970 between Britain and Argentina and so used in conversation in the colony.
Sulivan House	Official residence of Colonial Secretary named after Lieutenant Sulivan of the Royal Navy

Preface

These memoirs were written shortly after the author's husband, J. A. Jones, OBE completed a three-year posting to the Falkland Islands and Dependencies as Colonial Secretary. They were then placed in the archives of the Rhodes House Library in Oxford where for years they lay gathering dust. So remote was this British colonial outpost from most people's experience, or even consciousness, that when the question of its sovereignty led Prime Minister Margaret Thatcher to declare war on Argentina, many people were suddenly found scrambling for their atlases. While the events described here took place a good decade before the outbreak of the Falklands War, the author casts considerable light on the disputed historical claims to the islands and the tensions and suspicions that culminated in the declaration of war on 2 April 1982.

Chapter 1
Prologue

The controversial affairs of Gibraltar and the Falkland Islands were, up to a few years ago, handled by the same department of the Foreign Office. At that time a parallel situation existed, exacerbated from time to time by the dictates and whims of tottering regimes, hot-headed nationalists and greedy news media. The respective claims of Spain and Argentina were celebrated with an annual airing at the General Assembly of the United Nations, where much hot air was circulated but without apparent results. The two colonies are still British and both have some aspects in common; each has a Government House with all the trappings inseparable from the old colonial era; each has naval and army representation; each has the problem of sovereignty; but there the resemblance ends.

One is near at hand on the European package tour circuit, whereas the other is out of sight and, it appears, out of mind in the South Atlantic. The man in the street (the one who says everything is fantastic) is *au fait* with the geography, inhabitants, *vino* and fish and chips of one. On the other hand, he is either a mine of misinformation or abysmally ignorant about every aspect of the life and people of the other, even to the colour of their skins and, unless posted there, is unlikely to sample mutton chops for breakfast. Thanks to his oracle, the TV set, he can become emotionally involved over the doorstop situation of Gibraltar, while little concerned about the fate of his Falkland Islands fellow countrymen, who, one must admit after examination of ethnic ties and analysis of blood groups, is, unlike Gibraltar's polyglot population, of pure British stock.

The political cloud over Gibraltar appears to be stormier and the situation one of stalemate, whereas there has been a rapprochement, albeit shaky, between the islands and their giant neighbour. Gibraltar is under blockade whereas the contact with Argentina, which began during our stay in the colony, and continued as a once weekly air service to the mainland.* It is a moot point whether Gibraltar still holds any strategic value as a naval base.

Although the Falkland Islands lost their importance to shipping with the opening of the Panama Canal, the colony is still useful as a staging post for naval and research vessels on their way south to the Antarctic. It also appears as if the British trawlermen have wakened up to the existence of the rich fishing grounds there. The Falkland Islands government has for some time been at pains to draw attention to the abundance of South Atlantic cod, but so far only the Russian fishing fleet has taken advantage of the facilities offered by the port of Stanley. The sole industry of the islands has always been sheep rearing for the wool crop. In addition to the promise of a breakthrough in alginates as a second string to the economy there may yet be a third if British fishermen are prepared to cast their nets upon the waters of the Antarctic and the Falkland Islands may once more be a place on the map.

Finally, Gibraltar may have its apes but the colony of the Falkland Islands has much more to offer to the naturalist and

* This route is no longer used.

conservationist, for in addition to the penguins, seals and sealions, there are many unique species of bird life.

Astounded at the lack of knowledge about these islands, when one is asked by reasonably educated people where they are, what is the size of the European community and how many hours does it take to reach – this latter question posed at a time when the only link with the outside world was the once monthly shipping service to Montevideo – I have felt the urgent need to fill in some of the gaps, even although the bleakness of the terrain and the phlegmatic nature of the islanders make less interesting reading for the armchair traveller than the more volatile Gibraltarian. Throughout I have endeavoured to give an unexaggerated account of an unsophisticated society more at odds with the elements than with politics. Through it also runs the thread of the painfully difficult and slow process of adjustment on the part of the islanders to the necessity of opening up communications with the mainland, the understandable apprehension of a small colony of 2000 in taking such an irretrievable step, the fear that Britain was prepared to abandon them, leaving them to the mercy of Argentina and that once the die was cast the fate of the islands would become inevitably linked with that of Argentina.

Britain has undertaken to build an airfield in the islands to replace the Argentine operated temporary airstrip but rising costs have already doubled the figures first thought of and the fulfilment of the promise is bound to loom as an increasing and irksome burden. The islanders, already suspicious of Britain's motives regarding the colony, are still apprehensive that they might be forced to rely on the goodwill of Argentina for much longer than anticipated. Peron's return to power has now added to the uncertainty of their fate. The final chapter has yet to be written.

Chapter 2

Changes in the Air

In my imagination I can smell the peat smoke, hear the gathering wind and the warning call of an irate loggerduck jealously guarding its territory, as my thoughts reach out nostalgically across the ocean to the tiny world of the Falkland Islands, no longer a place on its own but fast becoming part of the global world.

We had spent three years in these remote islands and had witnessed the defensive behaviour of the Kelpers, as the local people like to be called, a name derived from the abundance of kelp beds round those coasts. Loggerducks fight to the death to defend their territorial rights and I often wondered what would happen if the islanders were put to the same test. This is now less likely because the recent opening of a temporary airstrip has brought the isolation of the past to an end. This historic event took place on 10 November 1972 when the first Fokker Friendship flight arrived from Comodoro Rivadavia. This flight, by the Argentine air force's developmental airline, LADE, was unheralded and and its praises unsung; in fact it had little or no impact except on those immediately involved. There were no headlines, merely a few unobtrusive words tucked away in an obscure corner of a British daily paper.

No doubt, the Argentine government also deemed it wise to play down news on these controversial islands because of the embarrassing presence in Buenos Aires of ex-President Peron, which could bode ill for the future of the islands on account of his hard line and unenlightened policy towards the British colony. Whatever the reason, to anyone who has visited or lived in the Falklands, the news of the opening of the temporary airstrip had far-reaching implications. Henceforth, until 1975, the year envisaged for the fulfilment of the British government's intention to construct a permanent airfield on Cape Pembroke, near Stanley, the colony's capital, a 'Fokker Friendship', with limited all-up weight due to restricted runway length and difficult weather conditions and so carrying only 16 to 20 passengers, will arrive once weekly from Comodoro. Irrevocable, far reaching changes and problems would follow in the wake of this event. It is this that inspires me to endeavour to capture, before the memories fade, something of the unique way of life in those far flung islands 8000 and more miles from the motherland, deep in the South Atlantic; and, because of our close involvement in island affairs during my husband John's three-year tour of duty as Colonial Secretary, to comment on developments that are changing the face of the Falkland Islands.

The colony is one of a dwindling number of dependent territories in the commonwealth, so its raj belongs to the old colonial era unfamiliar to today's British public; before such customs become completely anachronistic it may be of interest to record the ambience of '*autres pays, autres moeurs*'. It is perhaps no surprise that many people are barely aware of the existence of one of the last outposts of the empire, let alone its geographical location. A good example of this is the pleased reaction of the wife of a burly Scots Marine sergeant posted to the Falklands who expected her huband 'hame fer the weekend', confusing them, as many people do who are unsure of their location, with the Shetlands, whose bleak, windswept beauty is similar to that of the Falklands. Many people are also either under the impression that the colony is independent, or alternatively that the British government is anxious to shift the burden of them onto Argentina. People are also often surprised that the islanders are of British descent and are English speaking: indeed, very few of them speak Spanish. People in Britain and Argentina exhibited amazement bordering on disbelief at my description of the mode of life imposed on the inhabitants by the rigorous climate, the peaty terrain, the isolation and consequent lack of amenities. Their hardships have forged an island character that is resourceful, self-reliant and ingenious. I am sure that these admirable qualities, allied to a keen sense of humour, will cushion the Falkland Islanders from the impact of the world outside.

The islands make a vivid, deep and lasting impression on all who visit their shores. Perhaps, setting the scene will inspire more people to go and linger there awhile as the colony enters a new era, an era many islanders regard with misgiving and apprehension, fearing that their haven will lose its mystique, its unique identity. However, I am certain that those who truly care about the fate of the islands and its people recognise that the opening up of communications with Argentina is the only commonsense solution.

The Falkland Islands no longer possess the strategic importance they once had as a coaling and repair station for the Royal Navy during the first and, to a lesser extent, the second world wars. Also, with the opening up of the Panama Canal, the sanctuary it once offered to the many ships which limped into the shelter of Port William and Stanley harbour after rounding Cape Horn is no longer needed. The remoteness of the islands, though lending enchantment, renders them difficult for Britain to defend and the non-rapprochement with Argentina has become an increasing emharrassment at each United Nations Annual General Assembly.

Economic factors were becoming increasingly important. Shipping was about to grind to a halt with the withdrawal by the Falkland Islands Company of its ship RMS *Darwin*, which for years past had sailed between Stanley and Montevideo, as had her predecessor the *Fitzroy*. The cost of living was beginning to soar as a result of rising prices and freight charges on goods brought from Britain by the MV *AES*, a Danish cargo vessel chartered by the Falkland Islands Company. As the shipping link with Uruguay was soon to be cut it was sensible to look to the mainland, as Argentina was euphemistically called during our sojourn in the Falklands (because 'Argentina' was considered a dirty word) and air transport through Argentina was looked upon as the answer to an economic and human problem.

In return, the islanders would benefit from speedy transport of urgent medical cases to the British hospital in Buenos Aires, a steady two-way flow of passenger traffic, ready access to various forms of expertise, regular visits to their parents by island schoolchildren on the mainland instead of the previous once yearly holidays, more frequent deliveries of mail and newspapers and, possibly, reduced freight charges, in addition to more variety at less expense on the daily menu.

Argentina's offer of technical courses for school leavers has greatly increased the potential for educational and job opportunities; the world is now their oyster. Subsidised air travel to South America means that many who have never left the islands can now do so with comparative ease and can take a look at the world outside and what it has to offer. For the first time newly weds can spend their honeymoon outside the islands. Stan Heathman, who was last in Britain 27 years ago, once told us that he would not make the journey again until he could do so by air. When he said this nothing could have seemed more unlikely, yet in 1973 he and his wife made the journey by air to visit relatives and spend a holiday in Britain.

John would never have claimed that the islands were his favourite place because, after the explosive energy and eagerness for education of Anglophone West Africa, he found the apathy of a remote backwater frustrating. However, the human and political aspects of the job fascinated him, especially after his recent experience of dealing with a somewhat similar situation of the Senegalo-Gambian problem, and constituted both the personal reason for his going to the islands as well as the challenge of the assignment. John would readily have agreed that I had a more affectionate and understanding attitude towards the Falkland Islands and their people. Whatever our differing outlook and opinions we will always be grateful to have had the opportunity to play a part in developing the historical pattern of the islands. It was an enriching and rewarding experience.

Chapter 3
Hollow Laughter

We had arrived from the Gambia in November 1968 and were spending part of our first winter leave for many years in Portugal, wondering what was next in store, when a letter arrived with news of a vacancy as Colonial Secretary of the Falkland Islands. Our immediate reaction was to dismiss it as a bad joke.

Shortly afterwards came the fracas of Lord Chalfont's visit to the colony and newspapers were full of the Falkland Islands' affair. With growing interest tinged with some amazement and apprehension we read about 'the problem' and the reaction of the islanders to the minister's visit. Emotional enthusiasm was whipped up by appeals for solidarity over the islands' local radio network and a feeling of bitterness and suspicion had eaten into the islanders' usual good humour. A large organised demonstration took place on Lord Chalfont's arrival in Stanley, at which placards and banners were displayed bearing the slogan 'Keep the Falklands British'. We heard more about it once *in situ*, where it made sense, but out of context it appeared as ludicrous and rather pathetic.

During Lord Chalfont's visit the colony's Executive Council accepted his assurance that the British government had been acting in good faith in having talks with Argentina and that if an understanding was reached it would be fully in keeping with the promise of no transfer of sovereignty against the wishes of the islanders, who were reassured but still suspicious, as were the dubious Tories. Angry scenes took place in the House of Commons with wild accusations from the opposition that the Labour government was selling the Falkland Islanders 'down the river'; and reiterations from the foreign secretary that there could be no handover of the Falkland Islands to Argentina against the wishes of the people. No one was completely convinced and rumour was rife that the British government had already given Argentina a firm impression that the Falkland Islands would be ceded and that, because of pressure, this had subsequently been made conditional on the wishes of the islanders. The islands then took on a more interesting aspect.

On our arrival in London it was gradually borne in on us that, like it or not, we were about to become involved, so we took up the challenge. Somewhat despondently, I packed away all my West African clothing and began to think in terms of anoraks and woollens. After years in tropical countries, neither of us in fact owned a winter wardrobe and so we were ill equipped for a sojourn in the South Atlantic. Like the Ides of March, letters arrived from the Falkland Islands with depressing news about hats, sheepskin coats, garden seeds, servants, or rather the lack of them, kettles and cats and so forth. By then it was too late anyway to add or subtract from the assortment of clothing we had acquired and both disliked, so we packed madly, hoping we had enough layers to keep out the unaccustomed wind and cold. As it turned out, I, in particular, was physically unprepared for the change of climate and no matter what I had packed it would have made not the slightest difference.

The newly-appointed Colonial Secretary, Mr J. A. Jones, left Southampton in mid-April 1969 on the French passenger liner, the *Pasteur*. I was to join him in Lisbon with the heavy loads, a mountain of suitcases brought down from our flat in Porto, at which he, manlike, looked askance. Knowing something by hearsay of ships and ports in South America, I was determined to have enough bedding and other essentials under my eye in the cabin to ensure that if the rest 'walked' we would at least have a survival kit. It turned out to have been a wise precaution because one of our trunks was broken into and rifled; most of the blankets and flannelette sheets essential for the antipodean climate were missing. I was insured but the theft was aggravating, particularly at the beginning of our venture into the wintry unknown.

Our cabin was luxurious and we felt pleasantly pampered as we crossed the ocean, basking in the sun and taking full advantage of the swimming pool in the knowledge that we would be unable to swim for some time to come. The waters around the Falkland Islands are icy cold and more than one sailor in his cups has slipped in to be buried later in Stanley cemetery – peat soil is said to preserve corpses.

After the magnificent panoramic display of Rio de Janeiro, where everything from the Sugarloaf Mountain to the Copacabana beach seemed larger than life, came the shanty towns of Santos, reminiscent of West Africa and contrasting strangely with the luxury of the beach hotel on Guaruja Island.

Then came the unexpectedly choppy crossing of the bay between Brazil and Uruguay: in unfavourable weather conditions, we were told, ships often bypassed Montevideo, going straight on to Buenos Aires, which would have been awkward, as at that time we were not allowed to set foot in Argentina because of the 'problem'. However, our luck held and on a fine afternoon we sailed up the River Plate past all the sinister looking sunken wrecks to be met by the agent, McLean & Stapledont and taken through the seedy back streets of the dock area to the Columbia Palace Hotel. Montevideo, the capital, has been described as one of the most beautiful go-ahead cities in South America at a time when Uruguay was considered to be the Switzerland of that vast continent. Now, a faded beauty with a sad, shabby decadence, a glimmer of its past glamour and grandeur is still noticeable in the style of its architecture, in the intimate little squares, in the magnificent sweep of the Rambla skirting the seafront, in the vintage cars and in the charm of its people, all clad in a mantle of nostalgia.

We were informed of a 48-hour delay because of bad weather to our departure for Stanley on RMS *Darwin*, the small 1792-ton ship which plied the 1000 miles between Stanley and Montevideo once a month carrying passengers and mail. We were to find out later that this was not an unusual occurrence. We were thankful for the respite, for it gave us time to organise our clothing for the next leg of the journey and afforded us an opportunity to get to know a little more about Montevideo, which at that time was the terminal for the islands' transport communications and to which serious hospital cases were sent. The British school at Montevideo, or Monte, as it was always known in the islands, was a popular choice for secondary schooling, as there was no opportunity for such on the islands. It meant that children were able to visit their parents once a year during the southern summer, whereas scholarship children attending school in Britain could only come every other year during the southern winter. Parents could also send parcels to their children in Monte via RMS *Darwin*. A boarding house run by the British school authorities was called Falkland House, though it was not solely for island children.

During our short stay we were impressed by the reaction of Uruguayans generally on hearing that we were bound for the Falkland Islands; Customs waved us through and shopkeepers were most helpful. One could tell there was a strong almost sentimental link with their island neighbours. We also took the opportunity to stock up with fruit, Salus mineral water, an excellent concentrated fresh lemon juice called 'Zum' and Cubano biscuits to settle our stomachs on the journey south.

Lady Haskard, the wife of the Governor of the Falkland Islands, had warned me about the difficulties of obtaining servants there, and as I knew that Government House had recently acquired a Uruguayan maid, this seemed an excellent opportunity to investigate the market and perhaps make tentative arrangements. An enquiry at the shipping agents, however, drew a blank and I was left with an uncomfortable feeling that I was being warned off. I subsequently discovered that the policy in the Falklands was not to import foreign labour where local workers could be found, although, strictly speaking, it was well-nigh impossible to find a full-time cook or maid; locally-employed part-time assistance was available at the predecimal rate of five shillings an hour. The policy was aggravating but understandable; my first problem had been encountered but not surmounted.

The next day, after *Darwin* had docked and disgorged its passengers, we met the outgoing Colonial Secretary and his wife on their way to a temporary posting to the British Virgin Islands. A member of the British embassy staff in Buenos Aires arrived for a briefing session with the two Colonial Secretaries, giving the impression that it was all very serious and cloak and daggerish, but with a hint of comic opera. Later that evening, in the dining room, we met our first Falkland Islanders, Captain Nigel Miller of RMS *Darwin* and the Pole-Evans family who farmed on behalf of the Waldrons at Port Howard. I was staggered to see they were all drinking enormous glasses of milk. Sensing my curiosity they told me that the milk in Uruguay was so good. As I slowly digested this piece of information an image of lean and hungry kine appeared before me like a mirage and at another table the outgoing Colonial Secretary and his wife were gleefully carving their way through a huge platter of baby beef – but more of that anon.

The following afternoon was D-day for departure by *Darwin*, which lay out in the anti-port. Our suitcases and heavy baggage, now lighter minus much bedding, had already been put on board and we foregathered on the quayside to be taken out by tender. More Falkland Islanders and semi-resident expatriates of the islands were also there and, with growing apprehension and some dismay, we studied the embarking passengers and their friends. During our last posting in the Gambia we had become accustomed to admiring the exotic Wolloff women. The scenery now looked a little dull and after our many years in West Africa everybody looked too white.

Peter Thain, the cheerful Scots second officer with twinkling eyes in a plump rosy face, welcomed us aboard. I was to see more of him later on 'camp trips' when he was always very helpful at hauling the ladies on and off oil drums. RMS *Darwin* was a pleasant surprise, particularly as we had been warned not to expect too much. Painted grey and white, the diminutive mailboat was spick and span and we were grateful for the comfort provided by the owner's roomy cabin with, praise be, its own bathroom. We were later to discover that the cabin had its drawbacks, as it was placed high up near the bridge well above the ship's centre of gravity where every movement was felt; however, this was preferable to being incarcerated in a small stuffy cabin below where engine and kitchen smells prevailed. The ship had obviously not been intended for a sub-Antarctic run and was so designed that if the crew felt comfortably warm, the passengers boiled and if the passengers were comfortable the crew froze. As the crew was always there they naturally had priority. We were luckier than some as we could counteract the heat by opening our portholes. The agents had thoughtfully welcomed us with a bunch of red carnations in the cabin and all our suitcases had been stashed away out of sight. We were soon to realise why.

During our stay on the islands two visiting Argentine journalists, describing the RMS *Darwin*, emphasised its quintessential Britishness. I disagreed with them because, although the food was inclined to be so, with broths, mutton hotpots and milk puddings to the fore – a foretaste of what was in store for us – most of the stewards and some of the crew were Uruguayans with a sprinkling of Chileans, which had the effect of counteracting this impression. The rather comic situation arose of ordering from a very British menu and hearing it translated into Spanish when shouted through the serving hatch to the galley behind. Certainly, *dos panceques* sounded more appetising than two pancakes, but I never did discover how they coped with mutton hotpot. I imagine it was turned into an ambiguous *cazuela*. I ordered in Spanish as the other progression struck me as illogical and I had the feeling that I was being regarded with grave suspicion – Spanish speaking – a spy in our midst!

When full to capacity, *Darwin* carried 40 passengers, but this being the onset of the southern winter, southbound passenger traffic was reduced to a minimum with maximum numbers sailing northward. We were a mere handful. While still in harbour I unpacked just sufficient for the journey and then went out on deck to explore. On the upper deck was a glass-sided shelter with bench seats and a fixed table, on top of which I was startled to see a large wreath. I sincerely hoped it was not an omen.

To sail the 1000 miles from Montevideo to Stanley was to sail back in time to a Rip Van Winkel atmosphere; to arrive was of necessity by RMS *Darwin*. At that time there was no other form of transport, unless you elected to undergo the long haul by the MV *AES*, the Danish cargo-cum-passenger ship chartered by the Falkland Islands Company to carry freight and parcel mail to the colony and remove its wool crop, the major portion of which belonged to the company, on its return journey. The wool was sold at auction in Britain. The islanders nicknamed the *AES* 'the elastic-sided ship' and christened by us the 'cargo cult ship'. It was small, about 1200 tons with accommodation for between 15 and 20 passengers and normally took a month to reach Stanley. The misnomers were due to the fact that the islanders and shop owners were always waiting for parcels and goods which were invariably on its next sailing. Apart from the *AES*, unless you were a VIP and thus entitled to be lifted by a British Antarctic Survey ship or by the Royal Navy during the season from Punta Arenas in the extreme south of Chile, *Darwin* was your fate. I used to tell new arrivals that they had not really arrived; such was *Darwin*'s reputation that they were evidently quite pleased not to have done so.

We sailed on 9 May past all those sunken wrecks where the *Graf Spee* had ended her career, with the high rise buildings of Montevideo slowly disappearing from view in the glow of the setting sun. Ray Clements, known to everyone on the islands as Clem, whom we had already met in the Colombia Palace Hotel, identified several well-known landmarks among the wrecks. He was the logistics officer for the British Antarctic Survey (BAS), which had its advance base in Stanley. Any visiting VIP arriving in UK clothing was soon decked out by Clem in Antarctic socks, boots and anorak for visits to the 'camp', which soon changed their image, the Falkland Islands being a great leveller. An ex-naval petty officer with a neat ginger beard beloved by that service, he had served down south on the bases as a FID, the name commonly given to personnel serving on the bases and arises from the initials of the earlier organisation, the Falkland Islands Dependencies Survey. Clem was a mine of information on anything and everything concerning the islands and we were soon picking his brains on what to expect.

When I mentioned to him that the wife of a former Governor had informed me that a raincoat was quite unnecessary and that she had never worn one, Clem laughed loudly and said: 'Of course she never wore one. She got straight into the GH taxi at the front door and seldom went out otherwise.' Clem had been in Monte for hospital treatment, but his Scots wife Sadie, a competent shorthand typist who had worked for the BAS before her marriage, was still in Stanley. She had a part-time job at the Secretariat and had worked for the previous Colonial Secretary. Clem said, 'Sadie is waiting to pass judgment. If she likes the look of you she might work for you but if she doesn't she won't.' John was relieved to find later that he had passed the test and that Sadie would continue until her expected baby was almost due. There was often a dearth of secretarial staff in Stanley and as what was available was usually part time, John had to do much of his own typing.

We had already met Captain Nigel Miller in the hotel and renewed this acquaintance at dinner that first evening on board. He had attended school in Santiago before joining the Merchant Navy and was one of the few fluent Spanish-speaking islanders. As soon as the opportunity arose he returned to the islands to work for Darwin Shipping Company, a subsidiary of the Falkland Islands Company. When we reached the colony his father, Sidney Miller, had just retired as managers of Hill Cove Farm. Unlike his father, Nigel Miller was a reserved rather taciturn character, much given to making gloomy predictions about what could happen to the unwary in Monte.

Also at the captain's table were Dr Charles Galliemore and Mrs Margaret Luxton, who was returning to Stanley after a holiday with her daughter who was still at school in Britain. Mrs Luxton had been brought up in Montevideo where she had been a nursing sister in the British hospital. She told us that when she arrived in Stanley as a bride after a rough crossing, she told her husband that she would never again leave the islands.

Another fellow passenger was a 'camper', as people living in the farm settlements are called, and was returning from holiday in Montevideo after a tour of duty as a cook in the bunkhouse of one of the settlements. He generally wore slacks and a blazer with the Falkland Islands' crest and motto, 'DESIRE THE RIGHT', emblazoned on the breast pocket. He regaled us, in the glass sided shelter on the top deck, with stories of life in camp. It was our introduction to the island accent, which I found flat and ugly. When I showed some interest in penguin eggs he said: 'I always send some in every year to my granny in Stanley. I'll send you half a dozen too.' I did not pay too much attention as he looked too old to have a grandmother, but, true to his word, half a dozen eggs did arrive neatly packed in a cardboard box delivered by hand from the camp.

This same passenger was later convicted of rape and spent a considerable time in the Stanley gaol. On release he obtained a temporary job as a cook on the MV *Forrest*, a small 100-ton government-owned vessel which carried cargo and mail round the islands under the able command of Jack Sollis. The next time I bumped into the erstwhile cook on the government jetty in Stanley he greeted me cheerfully. There are occasionally cases of rape and incest on the islands, where, as in all small communities, some inbreeding is inevitable.

While on deck we were reminded of Sir Kenneth Bradley's description of his voyage to Stanley in the tiny *Fitzroy* and of the sound of island voices as we listened to the crew – 'red cheeked, blue jerseyed crew calling to each other in what sounded like a Berkshire accent,' though to us the accent sounded more like a cross between Australian and Rhodesian. The bosun was either Uruguayan or Chilean, as were several of the crew, so a form of Spanglish was often spoken. One member of the crew carried a birdcage around with him in which a canary twittered incessantly. Canaries were a popular buy in Monte and often found their way via the *Darwin* to colder climes to take up residence by kitchen Rayburns. We later discovered that the bird was a present for Stan and Mrs Heathman from their son, Tony, and so, like myself, was to find a home from home, but at that particular moment in limbo, I was contemplating our enforced sub-Antarctic migration.

Next morning we were relieved to find that our misery had been postponed; there was no noticeable movement and we spent the morning lolling in deckchairs, but by the late afternoon the wind freshened and from that moment onwards we were aware of the gradually dropping temperature. The skies grew grey and leaden and the sea sullen: the absence of land and shipping gave rise to the impression of sailing into a void, a feeling heightened by the uncanny silence of the following skuas, giant petrels and albatross, all wheeling and dipping and skimming the surface of the water with a slow beat of their giant wingspan as they merged like grey shadows with the sea and sky. The whistling of the wind intensified the eeriness, giving the impression of being a combination of a film set for the *Flying Dutchman* and/or *Ancient Mariner*. We spent hours admiring the grace and effortlessness of the Wandering Albatross performing sea-level aerobatics before, catching the windy upcurrents, it soared high above us. Occasionally, we caught a glimpse of a penguin streaking past among the wave caps, torpedo like, a revelation of speed and effortlessness in contrast with this bird's amusing clumsiness on land, as we were later to observe.

The new locum doctor, Charles Gallimore, who was also a keen bird watcher, often joined us at the ship's rail, his glasses slung round his neck and obviously enjoying the conditions. He was going out for six months while Dr Charlie Malone, one of the doctors at the King Edward Memorial Hospital in Stanley, was on leave and, as he was a bachelor, he was hoping that his fiancée, Patsy, would be able to join him in order to keep house. Patsy arrived later and to placate local convention went into digs with Orb Summers of the Woodbine shop. Patsy was one of those expatriates who thrived on a mutton diet. She arrived sylph-like and thin-faced and we watched her wax till her buxom departure, but admittedly looking years younger. Dr Gallimore, who was fair skinned, just grew ruddier with the wind.

That afternoon the engines stopped and the explanation of the wreath was revealed when a simple burial service took place for the former chief engineer. From the shelter on the top deck we held on tightly as the ship rolled and heaved during the short ceremony. The wreath floated momentarily, a gay spot of colour on the heaving grey sea. The feeling of desolation increased suddenly at the sadness of the occasion. Then we were on our way south again into an ever freshening wind. The ship was beginning to dance and we retired. Too late we remembered the thoughtful warning given about the round table in the cabin. As it waltzed dangerously round the cabin floor John intercepted it on its drunken journey and wedged it, as advised, upside down, in the corner of the settee. We lay completely disorientated.

The waters south–southwest of Montevideo are comparatively shallow and with progress towards the Roaring Forties and Furious Fifties a swell and bad weather are inevitable. *Darwin* had been built to carry cargo, but her holds were usually empty apart from mail bags. Consequently, once she had started to roll she seldom stopped until entering the Narrows, the entrance to Stanley harbour. She had in fact a horrid peculiar movement, a combination of a roll, a lurch, a sideways dance, a judder as the screw rose out of the water and raced furiously, ending with a sickening slap as she came crashing down again. The cross seas did nothing to help matters. The normal schedule for the journey was four days, but it frequently took longer and on one occasion nearly a week of misery had to be endured while she hove to for 36 hours in thirty- to forty-foot waves which broke the portholes of the lounge. I always had the greatest admiration for the crew and in particular for the stewards who, with feet asplay, valiantly carried trays to ailing passengers.

By the next evening the movement had abated somewhat and we were able to appear, a little unsteadily, to see a film about the islands, obviously shown for the benefit of the new Col. Sec. The theme of the film was the issue of the islands' sovereignty. On that occasion WE were the subject of propaganda, for this was undoubtedly a warning to 'KEEP THE FALKLANDS BRITISH'.

We were due in Stanley next afternoon but were delayed by heavy seas and did not arrive until late evening, by which time it was too dark to see anything but the dim outline of the land as we sailed through the Narrows and the twinkling lights of houses and street lamps climbing the hillside above the harbour. It was a comparatively mild evening with no wind and we were deceptively lulled by the calm. What looked like a taxi cab was waiting for us, flag flying, on the wooden jetty. It was the Government House vehicle, which actually was a converted London cab. We were driven along the seafront, again surprised by the absence of noise, and up the driveway to Government House. The Governor, Sir Cosmo Haskard and Lady Haskard were at the door to greet us and welcome us to the Falkland Islands. We had arrived. That evening I remember feeling very relieved when, on a whim, I unpacked our much travelled wireless and found the BBC. I felt a little less isolated.

Chapter 4
The Problem

Given that there has been so much hot and cold air raised over the controversial status of these wind-swept islands, a brief historical resumé should suffice. In 1493 a papal bull divided the known world between Portugal and Spain, thus providing historico–legal grounds for the Argentinian claim to the islands. The French mariner and explorer, Bougainville, founded the first colony there in 1764, which was named Les Iles Malouines after St Malo, the port from where the French expeditions set sail. The name was later Hispanicised to Las Islas Malvinas, which is how they are referred to today in Argentina and throughout South America. When Spain protested against the French occupation, France, recognising Spain's claim, evacuated the settlement at Port Louis. Then the 1810 revolution came and Spanish troops stationed on the islands left a year later. Till 1820, the islands were without any form of authority and were left to the mercy of whalers and sealers until Argentina, considering herself the inheritor of Spain's colony, claimed sovereignty and reoccupied the islands. Attempts at colonisation, however, were abortive until Louis Vernet, a naturalised South American, was granted concessions. He established a polyglot settlement from South America and in 1828 was appointed

Governor of the islands. Unfortunately for Vernet, a brush with the American sailing vessel *Harriet* led to the defeat of his garrison and the destruction of the settlement of Puerto Soledad by the United States naval corvette *Lexington*, in 1831, thus paving the way for the reoccupation by the British.

The British claim, which Argentina repudiates, is based on John Davis's discovery of the islands in 1592 when his vessel *Desire* was driven among them. The present-day coat of arms features his ship and the motto 'DESIRE THE RIGHT'. While the French were settling in East Falkland, a British expedition set out and reached the islands in January 1765, but the Spanish forced them to surrender their settlement of Port Egmont in 1770. A British expedition returned to the islands in 1771 but abandoned the settlement again three years later. However, when the British returned to the islands once more in 1832, they managed to reoccupy them unopposed. They took over the former Spanish settlement of Puerto Soledad and renamed it Port Louis. With only a handful of settlers at that time naval superintendents carried out the early administration, but in 1840 plans were made to colonise the islands. In 1842 Richard Moody arrived in the Falklands and in 1843 he became Governor and Commander-in-Chief of the settlement and Dependencies, with Port Louis as the seat of government. This was later moved to a new site in Port William and named Stanley, after Lord Stanley, Secretary of State for the colonies.

Over the years Argentina had continued to complain about the British occupation and in the mid-1950s President Peron revived his country's claim to sovereignty over the Falkland Islands and began the process of isolating the colony from the Argentine mainland. Many of the islanders' relatives had settled in Patagonia, but communication with them was maintained through the ham radio network and in this way touch was never lost.

The affair eventually came to a head when it was brought to the attention of the United Nations in 1964. On the very day when the question of the islands was to be raised on the agenda, the Argentine pilot and nationalist Fitzgerald flew singlehanded in a light plane to Stanley where he skilfully and daringly landed on the diminutive racecourse to plant an Argentine flag in protest against the British occupation of Las Malvinas. A furore developed over the incident and the outcome of the United Nations debate, which continued for several days, was a decree that Britain and Argentina should settle their differences forthwith. In 1965 the debate was renewed at the General Assembly; 94 voted in favour, 14 abstained and no one voted against the recommendation that Britain and Argentina should find a peaceful solution to the problem. On 14 January 1966, the British and Argentine embassies issued a communiqué in Buenos Aires restating their determination to seek a peaceful settlement by diplomatic means. Argentina, however, still wanted to reintegrate the islands and its people and in 1968 the Argentine claim was renewed. In Britain, public sympathy was aroused and there was strong opposition to such an idea in both political and financial circles, in particular from the Falkland Islands Company, which controlled both commerce and shipping and in addition owned at least 50 per cent of the land. Thus, it came to pass that in November 1968, when the Falkland Islands affair was brought to a head by Argentina's renewed claim to sovereignty, Lord Chalfont, minister of state in the Foreign and Commonwealth Office, was sent to Stanley to reassure the islanders of the British government's intentions.

Such, then, was the political situation awaiting us. One can hardly blame the people of the colony for being apprehensive, distrustful of new ideas, new faces and indeed of change of any kind. Their attitude had hardened and the very name Argentina was anathema. Children did not play at cowboys and Indians but at fighting the 'Argies', as they were locally known. After all, the political climate had been stormy for many years and a series of token invasions from the air did nothing to help; the most notorious of these was the 'Condor' invasion when a group of young revolutionaries hijacked an Argentine DC6 and forced it to land on Stanley racecourse. The group adopted the name Condor as illustrative of its purpose. The condor is a large vulture-like South American bird of prey, known in Argentina as the 'soaring spirit of the Andes' and the name has been evoked on many occasions during the last half century.

People seeing the plane circling low naturally thought it was in distress. They ran to help and as a result many of them were taken hostage, including some Marines who must have felt very embarassed. Another plane, chartered by the Argentine newspaper *Cronica*, crash-landed near Cape Pembroke during Lord Chalfont's visit and caused endless trouble because it had to he dismantled before it could be shipped by RMS *Darwin* to Montevideo for return to Argentina. These incidents all took place before our time, but I can appreciate how they coloured and hardened local attitudes towards Argentina. During our stay, people became agitated whenever a reconaissance plane flew over the islands and the elderly, in particular, would become very distressed until reassured by messages relayed over the local radio by the colony's government.

One fine afternoon, shortly before Governor Haskard's final departure from the islands, an aircraft appeared high over Stanley. It was unfortunately an Argentine reconaissance plane that had been blown off course, or had made a navigational error on its way to one of the Argentine bases in the Antarctic, or was deliberately having a look at 'the promised land'. Both Sir Cosmo and Lady H, as she was often called locally, were extremely angry at the intrusion, which they took as a deliberately provocative gesture and an insult, and an *en clair* telegram to the Foreign and Commonwealth Office was hastily dispatched. Many islanders were equally agitated and the radio telephone to the 'camp' was hot with messages. On the other hand, there were many who regarded the incident as a non-event.

The forceful and vocal demonstration held during Lord Chalfont's visit emanated from a genuine fear of a possible sellout to Argentina. As for the other side of the coin, it is little wonder that Argentinians become heated over their country's claim, for they have been indoctrinated since childhood into believing that the islands are rightfully theirs, and one does not need to look further than Ulster to recognise the power of such an ideology. The fact that *nuestras Malvinas* are British arouses passionately intense feelings. Argentinians are nationalistic in a deeply romantic way, probably conditioned by memories of their very bloody war of liberation. Many Argentinians grow up believing that the islands are populated by Spanish-speaking people held in colonial subjection by the British and longing for liberation. To digress, I discovered that many American tourists on the few big liners that call once a year at the captain's discretion, which really means weather permitting and safe for elderly passengers, suffer from the same delusion.

Argentinian school atlases use Spanish names for the islands and for most place names in the colony. For example, Stanley, often inaccurately named Port Stanley in English, is known to Argentinians and marked on Argentinian maps as Puerto Irigoyen after a former Argentine president. In Anglo–Argentine schools, where English textbooks are bought in bulk, expensive atlases have to be specially ordered to avoid 'the problem'. These schools follow two curricula, Spanish and English, and one's mind boggles at the thought of the ensuing confusion in geography classes. However, I was authoritatively informed that the subject is generally tactfully avoided.

From time to time, hardline Argentinian newspapers would stir up anti-British and anti-Falklands feeling. On one such occasion, when HMS *Endurance*, the Royal Navy's Antarctic patrol and research vessel, was paying its first visit to Buenos Aires, articles appeared about the pirate ship and the invasion of its pirate crew. Time and time again, these newspapers would raise the sovereignty issue, thereby creating waves of distrust among the islanders and inhibiting progress towards better relations.

For a considerable period after we arrived in the islands, Argentinian visitors continued to be *personas non grata*. If they applied for visas, reasons were found for not issuing them. Thus, the islanders had no idea what these foreigners were like; they had so far only seen the 'baddies'. It was considered unwise for Falkland Islanders and expatriates to pass through Argentina on their way from the colony on overseas leave in order to avoid what could be an international incident. Apart from the radio transmissions mentioned earlier, there had been no contact between the two peoples for many years. On a subsequent visit to Buenos Aires I discovered precisely the same situation, that nobody had any idea what the islands and its people were like and that they were avid for information.

There was a political stalemate – '*nuestras Malvinas*' versus 'Keep the Falklands British'. Both the Governor and the previous Colonial Secretary had been there for a considerable time, the latter for six years and the former for five. The Governor was to do another year's service in the colony at the request of the island's Executive Council to the Foreign and Commonwealth Office. They were consequently over involved; a breath of fresh air and new ideas and initiatives were required to break the impasse. People on both sides needed to rethink their positions. It was a delicate situation because, any slight suspicion of what the islanders considered brainwashing, they would baulk and retreat behind their 'British' façade. The benefits of association with Argentina had to be brought home to them but at the same time they needed constant reassurance that their rights and wishes regarding sovereignty would be respected and that their interests would be protected in every conceivable way.

It was a difficult task to accomplish within three years, though the difference between the situation at our arrival and our departure is, in retrospect, quite staggering. We arrived in South America unable to set foot in Argentina, yet our departure from the colony three years later was by amphibian aircraft, for the Argentine air force was by then running a regular, if interim fortnightly service. As the result of much painstakingly patient work by all those involved over the course of those three years, people's hardened attitudes gradually softened and they became more tolerant towards Argentina. The shrewd islander, by degrees, became aware that he could derive maximum benefit in return for minimum effort and, weighing up the pros and cons, he soon realised that if negotiations were conducted on his behalf in an intelligent way he would stand a good chance of getting the best of both worlds, British and Argentinian. In other words, he would probably be able to have his cake and eat it, and Falkland Islanders do enjoy their cake.

Before any meaningful negotiations could begin, each side had to be seen to be ready to make concessions. When we arrived the time was not yet ripe for normalising relations but we had not been involved. We were, in fact, for some time, regarded with suspicion. We had come fresh from the emergent countries of West Africa where John had worked for independent governments of the post-colonial era for a decade and I had taught in all-African secondary schools. The Kelpers found our background of close association with Africans difficult to appreciate, particularly in view of their pride in being an all-white colony; in fact, I had the impression that they felt this entitled them to special consideration.

Because I was able to help out in so many different ways, such as fielding Argentinian visitors from ministerial level downwards, translating documents and doing cypher work, I became more involved in John's job than is usual for most government wives. However, I found it fascinating and it gave me an interest beyond the battle with the Rayburn and concocting dishes to vary the monotonous mutton diet.

Chapter 5
Dire Straits

While the final adjustments were being made to refurbishing Sulivan House, the Colonial Secretary's residence, called after Lieutenant B. J. Sulivan, a naval officer who was sent to survey Port William and Stanley harbour in 1838 with a view to moving the seat of government from Port Louis, we were to stay two weeks in Government House. This was a rambling building of rather unfinished appearance due to the additions over the years of various wings of wood and brick construction by successive Governors according to their whims and the state of the economy. Nonetheless, it is an interesting house with several collectors' pieces of note, which include a small but valuable collection of books and manuscripts in the Governor's office. Outside the west wing of Government House stands a harpoon gun from Grytviken in South Georgia, the site of the former whaling station. A story is told of how the Governor and his wife, having heaved this heavy piece of ordnance into the desired position, discovered, to their horror, that there was still a live charge in the breach.

A pleasant, centrally heated, flower-filled conservatory extends almost the entire length of the north wall of the building, facing the sun and affording protection and a view across the lawn and inner harbour to Twelve O'Clock Mountain and the Camber. At one time a head gardener had been sent from Kew Gardens to tend the flowers, fruit trees, excellent vegetable gardens and greenhouses. Despite its sprawling appearance, Government House has surprisingly few bedrooms. We were allotted the Shackleton Room, a plaque on the door commemorating the fact that the explorer did in fact sleep there. According to Anne Henniker-Heaton's entertaining account in the 1971 issue of the *Falkland Islands Journal* of her girlhood reminiscences of Government House when her father was Governor, Shackleton is said to have remarked that the climate of the Falklands was worse than that of the Antarctic, a remark that was put down to the fact that that particular bedroom was the coldest in the house. I privately agreed with the illustrious gentleman. The passage leading to the room was known, for obvious reasons, as the Straits of Magellan.

The view from Shackleton Room the first morning certainly brought home to me that we were in the path of the Furious Fifties with the Roaring Forties and Howling Sixties in attendance. I was reminded that these winds could blow off the icecaps, round Cape Horn, and across the oceans, with nothing in their path between the islands and New Zealand. The weather had changed overnight and I watched with horror clouds building up and scudding across the leaden, lowering sky bringing violent squalls of driving hail and sleet, flurries of snow alternating with blinks of pale sunshine in unbelievable rapidity and all accompanied by savage blasts of icy, biting wind. Lady Haskard, who after five years was thoroughly acclimatised and obviously enjoying the conditions, drove John and me round Stanley in the Government House 'taxi'. As the cemetery was pointed out to us I, with visions of a large wreath before me, sat back and closed my eyes in an attempt to obliterate it and forget my forebodings.

John immediately became involved in Legislative and Executive Council meetings while I retreated into myself in a state of shock at the stark, bleak, drab monotony of the landscape and wild fury of the wind. Although I had been brought up on the southwest coast of Scotland, which might be considered a similar environment, any empathy had been dispelled by the combination of my West Indian ancestry and the aroma of Africa emanating from my parents' trunks. My first visit to Africa at the impressionable age of 16 had further whetted my appetite for tropical countries, to which I had gravitated as soon as I was qualified to earn my living. The traumatic shock I felt at such a change was in fact to last several months throughout the first winter while I adjusted to a way of life which was utterly alien to anything I had previously encountered. During this period I spoke little, needing all my energy merely to exist. Once the initial shock had worn off I was able to see beauty in the stark simplicity, the economy of colour and to become gradually reconciled to the rigours of the climate, taking pleasure in the varied wildlife, the peacefulness and solitude until eventually the islands and people won their place in my affections. During those first few months, however, I was like a zombie, with a bloodcount to match the temperature. It was cultural shock in reverse. I roused myself at dinner and cocktail parties held for us at Government House, but the procession of Kelpers and expatriates remained in the middle distance; and I was too dazed for any hierarchy to fall into place.

Some vivid cameos stand out from our stay in Government House. One is of mountains of food being consumed and urged on me by Lady Haskard with dire warnings about what would happen if I did not eat to counteract the cold. 'Dear God', I thought, 'is that amount really necessary to wellbeing?' Most incoming expatriates obviously thought it was; I was to contemplate many a new arrival waxing but seldom waning on the Falklands' diet. Another vignette is of myself struggling up Little Italy, where the bulk of expatriates live, to Sulivan House to inspect progress by painters and carpenters, a distance of much less than half a mile and the sheer shock of walking into an icy wind which cut like a knife and of arriving gasping for breath, horrified at the loss of energy in walking such a short distance. The snow-clad Twin Sisters hills ahead were no doubt a picture, but blinded by the keen wind I was in no mood to admire the view. I remember the sense of relief I felt in finding that Sulivan House was warm if the wind was in the right direction and had a certain shabby charm.

Stan Heathman, the kindly gardener-cum-handyman attached to Sulivan House was there to greet me and I could tell we would get on well together. He was a former shepherd who had come out from Somerset as a young man and had married a Falkland Islander. Apart from the war years when he returned to Britain to join the army, he had spent a lifetime shepherding in the islands. There was no aspect of camp life he had not experienced and was full of amusing anecdotes.

Yet another flashback is of the May Ball in the Town Hall on a teeth-chattering evening; this was a grand social event held annually and attended by All-Stanley, with the local debs in their first long white evening gowns. Later in the evening the May Queen was chosen by male vote and had the doubtful honour of being bussed by the Governor. The ball had an old-fashioned flavour with the Valeta, Military two-step, Gay Gordons, Waltz country dance and Eightsome reel obviously the most popular numbers, not to mention the islands' national dance, the Circassian Circle. Lady Haskard had already introduced John to its intricacies in the Government House drawingroom and there was no escape for the poor man. With some sympathy I watched as he, more accustomed to a West

African highlife, was pushed through his paces by a determined Governor's wife. Next evening was Prince Charming's turn. However, HE was not in the habit of attending this function and we were fortunately excused the privilege. After our hectic social round of introductions we retired thankfully to Shackleton's draughty abode and so to bed.

Once established in Sulivan House with my familiar objects unpacked, life became more normal until the weather deteriorated. (Was it possible?) It was in fact the onset of the worst winter for more than 35 years. Snow fell and lay in deep drifts, which was unusual in the islands where it could be guaranteed to snow or hail every month of the year, summer included, but seldom to any great depth and it usually melted quite quickly. That winter the Marines were able to use their skis, which are standard issue for a Falkland Islands posting but which usually return with them to Britain in pristine condition. I had not included Wellington boots in my new winter wardrobe and there was not a single pair in a small size to be had in the whole of Stanley. On that occasion I was housed for a fortnight. Another item I had not packed was hardware, having been assured that I would find any amount of pots and pans in Stanley shops. Ah! That cargo cult ship! Government House kitchen had to be dredged to produce on loan for five months a battered collection of museum pieces.

During that bad winter a disastrous flu epidemic hit Stanley and the local population went down like ninepins. We were to find that despite the purity of the pollution-free atmosphere, colds, coughs and stomach germs were rife. The local inhabitants had little or no resistance to infection imported from Montevideo by the *Darwin*, or from Britain by the *AES*, and were never able to build up an immunity. Both Stan and his daughter Jenny, who was helping out in the house prior to her wedding, were hit by this particularly virulent form of flu and

1. Sulivan House: the colonial secretary's residence.

were not seen for three weeks, while John and I were left to cope with the as yet unaccustomed mores of Sulivan House. Then I succumbed and retired to bed where John joined me later that morning.

It had been impressed on me that you *never* let your Rayburn out except for cleaning by the sweep, which was obligatory every three months because of chimney fire hazards. Houses in the islands are constructed mostly of wood and are liable to go up in flames like tinderboxes and there have been several disastrous fires when inmates lost everything but the clothes they wore. I had a bad fright one lunch time when our kitchen chimney caught alight; it had gone over its time for sweeping by about ten days because Sonny Morrison, the sweep, was in hospital.

As I was expecting John with two visiting Argentinian diplomats, Carlos Louge and Colonel Luis Balcarce for lunch, I had asked Stan to rev up the oven for me before he went off to his own lunch so that my baked potatoes would be ready in time. I had just checked that everything was ready for my guests and was about to dash upstairs to make myself glamorous when I heard an ominous roar and saw clouds of smoke belching past the windows. My friend Elizabeth Hughes, the dentist's wife, spotted me through the window and made vague gestures towards the roof. I then, in desperation, phoned Stan. Mrs Heathman answered my call. In response to my query as to how it looked from their cottage she told me 'Plenty of flames. Better phone for the fire brigade.' The Falkland Islands Defence Force kept its guns and ammunition in a large walk-in cupboard under the stairs – hence my anxiety. Having phoned my SOS I phoned John to tell him not to come home for at least an hour. Ted Clapp and his helpers were soon on the spot in their fine modern fire engine and pumping furiously up the chimney with Ted every now and then anxiously peering into my mirror, which he held to the opening at the back of the Rayburn. The chimney was by then dangerously hot and surrounded by so much wood I began to wonder whether to rescue my jewellery or my fur coat. However, all ended well except for the mess in the kitchen and we were able to sit down to lunch only an hour late. When I eventually remembered the potatoes it was to find a sad charred mess in the oven.

I knew that with Stan absent, I did not know enough about a peat-fired Rayburn to dare let it get too low as I would never be able to resuscitate it. I can still recall the nightmare experience of crawling feverishly up and down stairs to the Rayburn, our only source of hot water and of heat in the kitchen while making hot drinks and refilling hot water bottles. I had not as yet had time to come to grips with 'the monster' whose maw had to be constantly kept filled with vast quantities of peat sods, which were consumed with voracious ferocity. Later I was to become expert in banking the Rayburn so that the fire stayed in all night, but at that time I had still to learn its idiosyncracies. All in all, with such a chapter of accidents, it was not an auspicious beginning to our three-year tour.

Once Stanley had recovered from its epidemic, life returned to its wintry normal. This was when activities were at a low ebb and the islands closed down for the winter. That year, because the *Darwin* had to go into drydock in Montevideo, we were without mail, newspapers and passenger traffic for more than two months and our isolation was complete. We were introduced to southern winter highlights such as the drunken midwinter BAS party when messages, which were usually rude, were relayed to the bases where similar parties, minus the female office staff, were being held and functions such as the winter show took place with a fine display of artistic, gardening and culinary talent. There are many keen amateur artists in the colony and entries are of quite a high standard.

Hobbies such as gardening and baking speak for themselves as in order to eat fresh vegetables gardening is a necessity, as are the baking sessions for the many teabreaks, or smokos, as they are locally called. Competition in this field was exceptionally fierce and serried rows of carbohydrate fare vied with pots of diddle-dee jam and rhubarb chutney. The only baker in Stanley, Dobbyns, made good brown and white bread and cakes for special occasions with delivery twice a week by Land Rover, but most housewives in the Falkland Islands preferred to bake their own bread and are invariably wedded to their

Rayburns every morning as they listen to music relayed over 'The Box', as the local radio is called, or tune in to listen to the camp gossip on the radio telephone waveband. This popular pastime consequently meant nothing in the islands ever remained private.

Intricate and beautifully worked horse gear and horn carvings were usually sent in as exhibits from camp and were of exceptionally high quality. This hobby had been handed down from generation to generation from the time of the gauchos and campers spent many a long winter's evening practising these arts. Lelman, who was the handicrafts teacher on the staff of the Stanley schools and an islander, gave lessons in the craft, one of his more able pupils being the Governor's wife. The carpentry, dressmaking and embroidery sections of the winter show were also of exceptionally high quality with entries from old and young alike. One remarkable exhibit was a scale model, entirely handmade, of an old-fashioned spinning wheel. It was craftmanship of a high order and was exhibited by Clem of BAS.

This was also the time when the farm managers' wives descended on Stanley for a shopping spree while their husbands attended Sheepowners' Association meetings and reached their annual agreement in negotiations with the General Employers' Union whose secretary, Major Richard Goss, OBE, was an elected member of both the Executive and Legislative Councils.

At last, with Stan's help, I began to make friends with the Rayburn and would pore over recipes in an attempt to disguise the flavour of mutton, a task well-nigh impossible due to its venerable age. Most recipes began with the phrase 'Ask your butcher … to joint and point your mutton cutlets.' Such advice was only grist to the mill, there being no butcher in the accepted sense of the term. Mutton is known as 365 because it is literally consumed every day of the year and in the camp, where the day often begins at 5 a.m., mutton chops for breakfast, after a morning's work, featured in the daily menu, perhaps accompanied by 'buggers to float'. This delicacy is a type of dough, which someone at one time obviously had difficulty cooking. There is little variety in the islanders' fare, even at Christmas when lamb is the traditional dish accompanied by the ubiquitous turnip and the first new potatoes boiled with sprigs of mint, which grows like a weed in most gardens.

When I was still very new to island life I enquired politely if it were possible to buy lamb chops, but soon realised why Stan guffawed loudly. The butcher's van delivered mutton carcasses twice weekly, usually by the half or quarter carcass. The meat is hung on a hook in a large flyscreen netted safe, which is a feature of every household outside the back door by the kitchen usually facing south and consequently very cold. Every family owns a saw for hacking and doing its own butchery. No mutton lovers at the best of times, we both soon sickened of the rank flavour of seven-year-old sheep. After six months John went on strike and I, by then nauseated by the smell of raw mutton, gladly put away my recipes. Ask your butcher indeed! We had had our fill of meatloaf, meat balls, kebabs, shepherd's pie and so forth, in fact all 365. 'No meat today' became our motto. Most houses had, fastened on the garden fence or gate, a wooden board on which were painted instructions about mutton deliveries. 'No meat today' on one side and on the other 'Fore quarter please', or whatever. Food indeed was to prove a problem.

Since leaving the islands, I have often been asked how I passed my time there and my description of the daily routine was usually met by an uncomprehending stare. People accustomed to modern amenities seem unable to envisage a place where one cannot buy a newspaper, or pop round the corner to the fishmonger, butcher or grocer to buy something out of the deepfreeze; they find it difficult to imagine living in a place where it is impossible to turn on the television because there is none, where the need to stock up with enough butter and cheese for a siege becomes of paramount importance and the arrival of the *AES* with fresh stocks of boots, cosmetics or stockings, the bright spot on the horizon. There was a complete lack of amenities in the Falkland Islands.

Newspapers, if of the airmail variety, arrived by *Darwin* in vast bundles containing anything up to a month's issues, while the the ordinary editions had to wait for the *AES*. The only local papers were the *Falkland Islands Review* and various newsheets issued by church authorities, all of which were merely pamphlets on local affairs.

There are no fishermen by profession in the colony, no doubt because the seas are very dangerous and people prefer to work the land. Instead, one listened for the rare announcement on 'The Box', always introduced by the same martial music, to inform housewives that Micky Clark had mullet or smelt for sale at the corner of John Street. Both fish made excellent eating when available. People would then dash off in their Land Rovers, equipped with buckets, in order to fill up their deepfreezer. Contrary to what one might expect, the islanders enjoy a high standard of living and their houses are stocked with electrical appliances of every kind. Most families owned at least one large deepfreeze, but they were in a position to build up their stocks gradually. Catering was more difficult for people like us, who had to start from scratch without any reserves, and it took us all our time to fill the small deepfreeze cabinet at the top of our fridge.

Unfortunately, the Russians, with their huge factory-cum-research vessels and accompanying trawling fleets, have captured the South Atlantic market where they fish for Atlantic cod and other fine varieties off the islands as well as further south in the area of the Scotia Sea. They spend the entire year there, rotating individual ships at regular intervals. They were frequent visitors to Stanley harbour to take on water and mutton carcasses, and to offload an odd sailor to the small hospital to which they would generously contribute frozen fish in order to vary the hospital diet.

When in port, the Russian crews were allowed ashore for relaxation and they could be seen walking about Stanley in groups. They were obviously under orders to behave impeccably and in a friendly manner and the captain was under instruction to ensure that no unfortunate incidents occurred. Football matches with local teams were a regular feature of these visits as were film shows given by the visitors in the parish hall. The Russian factory ships carried a number of women crew members as stewardesses, cooks and research scientists. The captain and chief scientist would be invited to Government House lunch parties, but these occasions were exceptionally heavy going because of the language difficulty. Captain Petukhov could be observed sweating visibly with the strain of his efforts to make polite conversation. I usually found that the chief scientist had done a tour of duty in Cuba, so I was able to converse with him in Spanish.

On one occasion our interest in krill, the tiny shrimplike creature on which whales feed, led Captain Petukhov to invite us and Les Gleadell, the colonial treasurer and his wife, on board the *Akademik Knipovich* for a marathon lunch session. Captain Petukhov, our host, was a round, swarthy Georgian with a delightful sense of humour, in contrast with his more silent and reserved senior scientist. Served with pieces of good coarse bread and washed down with well-chilled vodka, the krill, which is of the consistency of a first-class paté, was either mixed with butter or cheese or simply served in its natural state. There were also ample supplies of black and red caviar, which, we were told, was served only on special occasions. Captain Petukhov told us that an attempt was being made in Russia to introduce krill to the Russian market and to use it as a source of protein for undeveloped countries. He said that five million tons of processed krill were consumed in his country each year and he took us out on deck to show us the fine mesh of the trawl used for harvesting this rich food. When one reads about the cod war off Iceland, one wonders why British trawlermen, who defend their fishing rights so belligerently, lack the spirit of adventure to go further afield to the South Atlantic, making the British colony their base. Perhaps their owners are not prepared to risk their capital so far from home.

The lack of variety in meat presented the housewife with another problem. Unless one lived in the camp or had relations there one seldom tasted the sweet flavour of the local steak, for cattle were killed infrequently and usually only during the winter months. The stark wooden gallows near the shoreline for hanging beef carcasses are a feature of every camp settlement. The first time I was faced with a quarter of the animal being deposited on my kitchen table, my reaction was to say 'take it away'. However, Stan responded to my SOS and, arriving from Dolphin Cottage, he was soon sawing away happily. After the deepfreezes are filled up the surplus is usually put in the pickle barrel, another feature of an islander's home, where lumps of meat are preserved in brine.

Liver was unfortunately banned because of a campaign to eradicate hydatid disease and was condemned and destroyed in the butchery's incinerator. From time to time in the past, half-hearted attempts were made to stamp out the disease, but since no one took it seriously and so did not cooperate, it continued to be a problem. The campaign did not get off the ground until a visiting agricultural team, with Terry McRea as the veterinary member, became involved. As a result of their advice the Falkland Islands government was able to impress on the population the danger of the disease to both animals and humans; information material in the form of posters and films was distributed and measures such as the regular dosing of dogs were made compulsory. So far, there have been remarkably few human cases of the disease and these have been sent for treatment to the British hospital in Montevideo. Treatment can involve incapacitating surgery and after some such cases the campaign gathered impetus.

The islands have, happily, always been free of foot and mouth disease, but while there are regulations that contribute to this situation it is also due in considerable measure to the colony's geographical isolation. Measures exist to prevent fowl pest from which the islands have suffered disastrously on at least one occasion. I recall that an outbreak of this disease in Uruguay caused *Darwin*, on one of its southbound voyages, to hurl overboard anything connected with a hen, compensation being paid by the Colony Government.

Because of the humane method the abbatoir employs to kill sheep, it is almost impossible to obtain brains, for the brain would be spoiled and the heads thrown into the sea for the scavenging gulls. Occasionally, if Stan thought we were looking starved, he would cycle up to the butchery to split open a few heads, returning spattered with blood but with a rare treat for us in a bucket. I only once saw a sweetbread, which was donated by Mrs Heathman. We were always very grateful and appreciative of her excellent brawn, which she made from the cow hoofs and houghs which her son brought in from the camp. Kidneys were by kind permission of Stan and his cat, as to acquire them you needed to buy the hindquarter of the animal. Islanders seldom eat offal, which they regard as cat food.

There is no greengrocer from which to buy fruit and vegetables. Instead, you grow your own vegetables, which are mostly of the root variety, and import a crate of fruit from Monte on the once monthly *Darwin* sailing; various consortia were formed to cut down on freight charges. The monthly treaure trove lacked variety, as it often consisted of tangerines and oranges with the occasional addition of tomatoes, grapefruit, pimento and bananas, which either arrived green or over ripe. On one occasion a large cabbage was included, but not appreciated; I sent off a gentle reminder to the agents about sending coals to Newcastle.

Equally, there are no shoemakers. Shoes in need of repair had to be sent to Monte on the *Darwin*, or worn until they were thrown on the scrapheap to be replaced by new ones – the *AES* and Falkland Islands Company permitting. It was always wise to keep at least one pair in reserve. Nor were there any drycleaners. Again, clothes had to be sent to Monte, a doubtful procedure, and many a garment with advice to dryclean on its label, found its way into the washtub. The Falkland Islands is definitely a do-it-yourself place that takes up lots of time and energy.

Planning meals to vary the diet also took toll of one's imagination and to achieve success we had perforce to resort to expensive tinned food imported from Britain. I was to discover that tinned chicken disguised tastes well and that tinned tuna made the best fish cakes. Islanders do keep hens, but mostly for their eggs – that hen might just lay one more egg, by which time it is too old and tough for the pot. Each household has a large drum full of dozens of pickled eggs for the winter months when the hens stop laying. Fortunately, Stan had super hens and was able to keep us supplied throughout the year with half a dozen eggs a week, so we were able to keep our pickled eggs for baking purposes only. In fact, I sold several dozen before we left to a newly arrived married couple who were glad to acquire a small reserve. Stan's free-range hens produced some of the best eggs we have ever tasted.

Locally cured bacon could not be obtained as is customary in most farming communities. A few settlements had experimented with rearing pigs, but their attempts had been unsuccessful as the pigs were fed on mutton scraps and so tasted of 365.

Hares were occasionally shot, but always outside Stanley as legislation had recently been passed giving them protection over the whole area of Stanley Common. The legislation also covered birds and the visible increase in their numbers in the Stanley area during our three-year stay was proof of its efficacy. We were able to judge the effect with accuracy because the piece of legislation in question was passed at the first Legislative Council meeting held after John's arrival in the colony, which was within a month of our arrival.

Campers in the settlements fared better with their food because, although they had to bake their own bread and churn their own butter, cattle and young sheep were at least culled for consumption. Campers also had the advantage of being able to shoot game for the pot. There were plenty of teal, duck and widgeon in season as well as large numbers of Upland Geese throughout the year. The farmers regard these geese as a pest because five of them crop as much grass as one sheep and the government pays five pence for a beak. They are fine looking, prettily marked birds in soft browns and greys. They also make good eating, particularly when young and feeding on the new oat crop, which gives them an excellent flavour. A local speciality at this time is goose pie. Old birds are inclined to be dry and need to be well doctored with red wine, but whatever their age they made a welcome change to our diet. Upland Goose feathers make excellent brushes for sweeping up peat dust and no household is ever without several. Lest the conservationists be worried at these facts, I add that these birds can be numbered in their hundreds of thousands in the colony and there are no plans to exterminate them.

Once a year reindeer were sent up on a BAS ship from South Georgia where they were culled because their growing numbers were becoming a nuisance. Their meat had a more delicate flavour than venison and made a real gourmet meal. We preferred the ribs, for I was able to cut steaks from them, which I then grilled slowly in port wine. Another seasonal treat was the odd mushroom Stan found in the paddock at the back of Sulivan House. They were plentiful in parts of the camp where bucketsful could be collected and kitchens strung with them drying. In summer locals would go out to the Common and the fields beyond to gather the deep red clusters of diddle-dee berries to make jam and later in the season the Malvina tea berry. I bought some diddle-dee jam at a church bazaar, but found it too sickly sweet for my taste. It was, however, well suited to the islanders' sweet tooth.

As for milk, my picture of lean and hungry kine was not far off the mark. It varied in quantity and quality according to the time of year and state of the grass, and I must admit that the receptacles, an odd assortment of unsterilised orangeade, lemonade, gin and whisky bottles, placed on your milk in-tray by the garden gate were rather off putting. In summer the milk went off rapidly, despite boiling, so we switched to Marvel, leaving the milk tray free for our black cat visitor, which used to sit in it with a basilisk stare willing you to invite him into the summer warmth of the conservatory. Our visitor was a great hunter and could often be seen prowling round the house or teasing loggerducks, which were at least twice its size. Unlike most people in Stanley, who drank the local milk, we did not suffer from Stanley tummy, which was as endemic as gyppo tummy in other places, but neither did we drink the water, which was also not above suspicion.

After our years in West Africa, where the water had to be boiled, we preferred to import stocks of natural mineral water, called Salus, from Montevideo. Campers again fared better, as they always swore by their natural spring water and had the advantage of good milk on their doorsteps. There must be some truth in adaptation to environment, as the locals appeared to thrive on their mutton and root vegetable diet and produced very large babies as a result of their high protein intake. One's diet was supplemented in season by penguin and goose eggs, the former, with a bright orange yoke set in an enormous white, which I am told makes excellent meringues, has a very strong fishy flavour. Egging week is regarded today as a traditional custom. An annual holiday used to be held and the period is still known by that name.

Fortunately, Stan had green fingers and produced an excellent variety of vegetables for us. We became semi vegetarians. In winter I would make enormous pots of lentil or split pea soup, using every vegetable available in the garden, and to ensure we got our winter greens I learned to make a salad with the ever abundant kale as the basic ingredient. We discovered that fresh new turnip tops, though rather bitter in flavour, provided us with another green spinach-like vegetable, which I hoped was full of iron.

In summer, the garden would surprisingly come up trumps with gooseberries, raspberries, strawberries and redcurrants and in the late spring literally forests of rhubarb grew in profusion. Lettuce, parsley, spring onions and mint also grew well and we would fall on them like cows when the season came round, for by then we obviously lacked something in our diet. We were fortunate to have a large greenhouse where Stan grew excellent tomatoes, thanks to his horses.

2. Author in Sulivan House garden, beside a rare tree: *macracarpa*.

It was always amusing to see these four-legged lawnmowers at work in Stanley gardens and to be confronted by a horse's face peering over a garden hedge. The grass there is usually too coarse for a mowing machine, so when their owners bring the horses in from the camp where they spend the winter, they are farmed out to various gardens. I used to enjoy waking up to the clip clop of Stan's horses as they switched from one end of the garden to the other and to see Stan rushing out later with a shovel for their offering to the special brew he mixed in a large oil drum outside the greenhouse. This was a real labour of love on Stan's part because he did not actually like tomatoes and never ate them. Nevertheless, he guarded them jealously and woe betide John if he began to pick them too soon!

Gardens are always enclosed behind stone dykes, or by wooden fencing against which gorse grows, to protect them from the searing, swirling effect of the wind. The vegetable gardens are then further squared off by more box or gorse hedges affording added protection. Despite these precautions, the wind and driving rain could still wreak havoc, with the swirling wind uprooting newly planted or growing vegetables and the sea spray spoiling a good crop. Gardeners are frequently unlucky with their potato crop, as this is often hit by blight, but carrots and turnips usually withstand the elements.

Cabbages were inclined to shoot, carrots to cork and cauliflowers to fail completely. One feather in Stan's cap during our last year was to produce, after some trial and error, the first ever crop of broccoli in the Sulivan House garden. Broccoli, for some reason, is a particularly capricious crop in Stanley, growing in one or two gardens only. Onions did not grow at all and had to be imported from Montevideo. The vegetables had a good flavour, but unless replenished regularly, the peaty soil was impoverished and so the minerals necessary to one's diet were probably missing.

The shops had very little cold storage space and this was usually reserved for butter, cheese, packets of bacon and ice cream, but fortunately they did stock dehydrated vegetables and fruit such as dried apple rings to fill the gap. It was necessary, I found, to reorientate all one's ideas about food and shopping, stashing away whole cheeses, mountains of butter and margarine and tins of Marvel galore while they were available, buying Wilkinson's Sword razor blades by the gross and wireless batteries by the dozen. There was often a shortage of the latter because the *Darwin*'s crew members found a ready

3. Stan Heathman with 'lawnmower' outside Sulivan House.

market for them in Montevideo and whenever Stan was running out of them, he would put them in the oven to bake. Our large fridge became a store cupboard placed as it was in a very cold pantry, which was almost a fridge in itself, it was seldom necessary to turn it higher than the minimum setting. Some people have expressed surprise that fridges and deepfreezes were used in that climate and, indeed, had one been able to buy what you wanted when you wanted in a store or market, they would have been superfluous.

I normally did my shopping in the morning and used to wonder why the streets and shops were so deserted until I discovered the morning routine of the housewives baking madly to keep their tins full. Falkland Islanders spend a lot of time eating and have a meal or snack every three or so hours, starting with tea and biscuits around 6.00 a.m. for people in Stanley and even earlier in the camp, followed by breakfast at 8.00, smoko at 10.30 with tea and carbohydrates, lunch around midday off the inevitable joint of mutton surrounded by potatoes and other root vegetables, followed by another smoko at 3.30, supper at 6.00 of cold mutton and a final snack for good measure at about 9.00 p.m. In between times, the islanders, all of whom have a very sweet tooth, consume large quantities of sweets and chocolates. Long lists of the latest imports of these items were relayed over The Box within a short time of the arrival of a new consignment.

The islanders also have a penchant for hard liquor and the pubs and clubs do a roaring trade in the evenings. There is a high rate of drunkenness to which the black book owes its existence. Any spouse can complain about his or her other half's state of inebriation and have the offender's name blacklisted; it then becomes illegal for anyone to serve that person with an alcoholic drink. Such heavy drinking is probably due to the hard life, the lack of culture and other amenities. A cinema is held in the Town Hall once a week and dances irregularly; whist drives are popular winter pastimes, there is no television and people have no opportunity for further education.

For the same reason, no doubt, the divorce rate is high and Stanley is one of the easiest places in which to obtain one. Perhaps it has a future as the Reno of the South Atlantic, though how anyone there has enough energy left for intrigue after gardening, cutting peat, baking, butchering and all their other activities, was always beyond my comprehension. An experimental mink farm established a few years before our arrival failed, according to the locals, because the mink could not breed in the rigorous climate!

One of John's many tasks as Colonial Secretary was to act as Judge in the Colony's Supreme Court, as the employment of a full-time judge could not be justified. The divorce rate dropped rapidly for a while after he granted alimony far in excess of what an islander normally reckoned to be a wife's worth.

Chapter 6

Mise-en-Scène

Stanley, the capital of the colony, named after Lord Stanley, Minister for the Colonies during the early colonisation of the islands, is a small town of approximately one thousand inhabitants, but is more like a village in appearance. Steep streets rejoicing in bizarre, euphonious names such as Hebe Street (locally pronounced Heeb) and Philomel Street, the names of naval vessels of long ago, climb the hillside in parallel, intersecting lines of regimental precision, as befits a town mapped out by the first military Governor of the colony, Richard Moody. The houses, with their pan roofs brightly painted in contrasting shades, provide a splash of hard colour against the drab pastel of the landscape with an almost Mediterranean gaiety.

Each house has a walled or fenced garden, some of which have been turned into miniature gnome-lands, where the hardier varieties of flowers such as lupins, pansies, bluebells, Icelandic poppies and daffodils grow in profusion behind the shelter provided by box hedges and other shrubs. Almost all have conservatories where more exotic pot plants, and even roses flourish. It is as if the people there had made a conscious effort to offset the monotony of the climate and landscape by adding splashes of colour, and they obviously take great pride in the neat appearance of their houses and gardens. In springtime the countryside is suddenly aglow with golden daffodils and gorse; it is as if a painter had suddenly gone berserk and started splashing daubs of bright mustard yellow paint everywhere in a sort of Tachiste frenzy. The gorse is not the dull muddy gold of the British variety, but has the glow of genuine burnished metal.

Backing most houses are vegetable gardens and hen runs, where fowls scratch among clumps of tussac grass and gulls perch on the rooftops awaiting their opportunity to fight over the mutton scraps thrown to the hens. Also at the back of each house you will find the permanent feature, the peat shed, an open slatted, wooden shed with a pan roof, built in such a way as to allow the peat to dry out thoroughly. Inside are neat stacks of peat sods and mounds of peat dust sufficient for a year's needs. One of the most pleasant things about this fuel, apart from its cheerful blaze, is the scent of peat smoke on a still night.

As you walk through the small town you come across general stores and small shops, such as the Falkland Islands Company's West Store, known locally as the FIC and in the Argentine as Fic, the Globe Store, Philomel Store, Kelper Store, Speedwell, Woodbine Shop and the Co-op, to mention a few. In fact, there is quite a large number, really, considering the size of the population.

There are two government school buildings in Stanley, a primary school in the centre of town and a senior one at the far end. There is no grammar school on the islands and the school leaving age is 15. By now, a new senior school building should have been completed to replace the one gutted by fire on a cold, winter's night of driving snow and high winds during our first year in the colony. Staff for both schools is recruited largely from Britain, though a few teachers are hired locally to swell the numbers. Children can sit a scholarship examination at the age of ten or eleven, but this is not compulsory and many islands children do not take advantage of the opportunity of further education in South America or Britain as their parents feel that they cannot afford the extra money involved, although both scholarships and government grants are generous.

Education for children in the settlements is provided for by a small boarding school at Darwin, which the government subsidises at considerable expense, the per capita cost working out at about £375 per annum in 1971. Itinerant teachers regularly travel round the settlements to visit those camp children who are unable to attend Darwin boarding school. They spend a week or two at each settlement in turn before moving on their rounds in the Government Air Service Beaver floatplane, living out of a suitcase and dependent on the hospitality of farm managers and farm workers, which is an unsatisfactory arrangement for teachers and pupils alike. These camp teachers are also recruited from Britain and a move is afoot to employ only qualified ones instead of the unqualified staff which is all that has been possible hitherto.

Near the junior school is the local broadcasting studio, which relays BBC news, radio newsreel and other vintage programmes each evening from 6.30 onwards, or from 7.30 in the summer. There are a number of hotels dotted about Stanley, which except for the Upland Goose, are really glorified pubs, including the Rose Hotel and the Globe Hotel. The latter is a favourite haunt of the Marines for their Sunday 'glory hour', so-called because the pubs are only open on that day from 12 noon to 1.00 p.m. From Sulivan House we used to view the covered wagon transporting silently sober Marines towards town. An hour later whoops and catcalls would herald their jubilant return journey to Moody Brook.

4. Stanley from the air (photo taken from a Beaver).

The Upland Goose, situated on the seafront and owned by Ning and Des King, is a small, pleasant, well-run little hotel with 12 bedrooms and room for expansion. Plans are afoot to instal more showers and toilets and the management looks forward to a bright future in tourism.

There is also an abundance of other bars, such as the Gluepot, and social clubs like the Falkland Islands Defence Force Club and the Workingmens' Social Club. There are flourishing clubs of a different nature like the football, cricket, golf, squash and badminton clubs and indoor and outdoor rifle clubs. Falkland Islanders are excellent shots and frequently win prizes at Bisley, as they are accustomed to shooting in climatic and wind conditions that are far worse than any they are likely to meet in Surrey. It is, however, too windy for tennis. For some years efforts were made to raise funds for a swimming pool, but despite a steady accumulation of contributions the total was never enough to counter the effects of inflation and the project has not yet got properly off the ground, despite it having been very close to our hearts.

There are churches of all three denominations. The cathedral, which is Anglican, the state religion, is an imposing spired building and ludicrously large for the size of the community. Adjoining it is the Garden of Remembrance with a rather tired looking whalebone arch and where daffodils fight for survival in the spring winds. Opposite the Town Hall is St Mary's, the Roman Catholic church where Monsignor Ireland presides. Monsignor had been a chaplain and had served with Montgomery in North Africa. Nearby is the Tabernacle, or Tab, as it is known locally. Both St Mary's and the cathedral have their own halls, where bazaars, whist drives and other social functions are periodically held, bazaars being the most popular and at which surprising amounts of money are spent. It is not unusual to hear an announcement on the islands radio, for example, that St Mary's had raised £2000. Snacks and meals would be served at these functions and since there were then no restaurants in Stanley this presented a golden opportunity to eat out for a change. The 'Roman Catholic restaurant' was the most popular because the lay brother, who had formerly been a professional chef, was an exceptionally good cook.

The Council Chamber, Town Hall, Post Office, Library, Museum and Legal Department are all housed under one roof. The Council Chamber is where the opening of the Legislative Council takes place, when the Governor appears in full rig, but this ceremony was seldom attended in any number by the community, a mere handful turning up, apart from one occasion when a group of stony-faced hardliners appeared for the reading of the president's address on the forthcoming policy towards Argentina. They looked grim and determined, but to my disappointment nothing untoward happened.

A once weekly cinema show is held in the Town Hall which is also the venue for wedding parties and dances. The Library and reading room are reasonably well stocked and open for a few hours every evening, except Sundays, but again it was not well attended by the local community, few of whom had much interest in such pursuits. The Museum houses a tiny but interesting collection of pieces from old sailing ships, as well as Fitzgerald's flag. It has recently been moved to a new site in the gymnasium and is ably run by John Smith, an authority on the old sailing ships which visited and many of which never left the islands. Next to the Council Chamber is the Legal Department where Harold Bennett and his clerk sit in state sorting out knotty problems. The Post Office deserves special mention because the staff there always worked like Trojans till all hours whenever the *Darwin* or *AES* delivered mail. When all the mail had been sorted and placed in people's private boxes, an announcement, heralded as usual by martial music, would be made on the local radio that letters were ready for collection, to be followed later by a similar announcement about parcels. People often received a backlog of several months' mail and their Post Office boxes would be full to overflowing. On such days there was a Christmas-like atmosphere as people dashed in and out of the Post Office. Near the Town Hall, on the opposite side of the road, is the Police Station, or Scotland Yard, as Stan christened it, ably run by Inspector Terry Peck, who had under him Sergeant Felton, a corporal, Toddy Macmillan, who was the local barber, and five constables.

The Public Works Department (PWD), with its many sheds and buildings where venerable old men of 90 still do odd jobs, is also at this end of town. There are three jetties in all in Stanley – the Government one, which is the home of the MV *Forrest* and Government Air Service, the Public jetty, which is notoriously windy and where normally BAS ships tie up and add to its tottering state, and the Falkland Islands Company jetty, where the *Darwin* and *AES* berth. Near each jetty is a conglomeration of dilipadated sheds, slipways and old hulks, the odd one of which is still used as a store.

A new industrial venture, the experimental plant of Alginate Industries Ltd, has been set up on the seafront near the offices of the Falkland Islands Company. The purpose of this pilot plant is to exploit kelp commercially, but because research needed to be undertaken into various problems, particularly the unusual stickiness of the islands' variety of the weed, a plant was established two years earlier under the supervision of Fred Gooch. In the process used in Scotland hundreds of thousands of gallons of fresh water are needed to process the raw material, but this requirement would be difficult, though not impossible, to meet near Stanley. Fortunately, it was found that seawater was more suitable for the purpose in the South Atlantic. Recently, there has been a breakthrough in processing which will allow the finished product to be made in the colony so that prospects for the establishment of a second main industry in the islands look bright.

Macrocystis pyrifera grows in profusion in the waters round the islands and has the peculiar property of regenerating itself twice as quickly as anywhere else. Its tree-like growth allows it to be harvested from specially designed boats and its properties are generally considered superior to the product from the weeds hitherto harvested in European seas. 'Tree-like' is an appropriate description because the *macrocystis* stem reaches the thickness of a man's leg. Viewed from the air as one flies round the islands the kelp sways and streams in the water like some dark forest of snakes and, in certain lights, has a copper red hue. The history of evaluating this resource in the colony is almost as lengthy as that of discovering an oil field, for the first surveys were made more than twenty years earlier. However, it is hoped that the wait has been worth while because the prospect, at last, of some diversification of the colony's monocrop economy, is most welcome. Every one who wishes this outpost of the Commonwealth well, must will the success of this venture.

At the western end of town, along the sea wall approaching Government House, is the Secretariat, a grey, faceless building, with the printing department behind it. The old Secretariat was burnt down not so many years ago and many files and papers were lost; some people say it was opportune, but with what truth and to what end I have never discovered.

Nearby is King Edward Memorial Hospital, a small, pleasant building with 40 beds. There are two doctors, a matron, several nursing sisters and an adequate number of nurses, but the hospital always has great difficulty attracting doctors and nursing sisters to work in so remote a place. The pay is insufficiently competitive with going rates in Britain or other parts of the Commonwealth. The nurses' home, which is close to the hospital, overlooks the football field. The hospital also serves as an old folks' home with its own sitting room, dining room and conservatory. Serious medical cases are sent to South America, previously to the British hospital in Montevideo but now to the British hospital in Buenos Aires.

Up the hill towards the common is the powerhouse, under the supervision of Ted Gutteridge, where sufficient electricity for Stanley is generated. In camp each settlement has its own generator and the lights come on each evening at dusk and are then switched off at 10.30 a.m.

A pleasant walk farther westwards along the sea wall takes you past the shags and loggerduck families to Government House, with the football field on on side and the offices of the British Antarctic Survey on the other. From here you walk through Little Italy, so-called because it is where the majority of expatriates live. It is also where the Battle Memorial, erected to commemorate the Battle of the Falkland Islands when Sir Robert Sturdee's battle cruisers defeated von Spee's fleet in the icy waters southeast of the colony, is to be found. It is an imposing monument, with cast plaques on each face, and, silhouetted against the skyline with a frieze of gorse in bloom, it makes an impressive sight. A parade is held annually on 8 December each year to commemorate this British victory, a month when the gorse is in full bloom.

Continuing along the sea wall or on the road up above you come to Sulivan House, in front of which is the old trading hulk the *Jhelum*, an East Indiaman, now the haunt of shags and night herons. The surfaced road continues in a westerly direction past the hangar in which the Falkland Islands Government Air Service's de Haviland Beavers are housed and past the butchery, to peter out at Moody Brook, the quarters of the Marine detachment, the Hovercraft unit and the naval party. Through the town in an easterly direction, the surfaced road comes to an abrupt halt just beyond thc cemetery.

On the other side of the harbour, where many old hulks and schooners lie at rest, is the Camber with its oil tanks and naval dockyard, behind which, on the hillside, the names of naval ships that have been frequent and popular visitors to the colony are etched in whitewashed stones. During our time in the colony the name of HMS *Endurance* was added to that of the *Protector* and *Beagle*. It was interesting to watch the naval helicopters buzzing to and fro, hovering low over the slopes as they offloaded their boulders while the naval working parties scurried around like ants, the name *Endurance* slowly taking shape.

The colony's population is approximately two thousand. The one thousand who live outside Stanley are scattered in settlements throughout the camp and they work principally as shepherds and farm labourers. A few years ago the experiment was tried of importing shepherdesses, mostly from Scotland, most of whom have since settled down, marrying islanders. The story goes that many arrived with the idea of taking a bus into Stanley at the weekend to see the bright lights of the capital, so they were somewhat taken aback to discover that there were no roads on the islands apart from the few miles from Moody Brook to the cemetery in Stanley.

Outside Stanley rough tracks take over and these lead over peaty, tussacy, bumpy and often boggy terrain; driving over such tracks in a Land Rover requires much effort and considerable skill and experience. Most people prefer to use the FIGAS Beavers, which, weather permitting, operate daily apart from Sunday like a taxi service. Because there are only some 12 miles of surfaced road in the entire colony there are very few cars; people finding the Land Rover a sturdy vehicle for rough driving and more useful for fishing excursions to the Murrel or Marlow Rivers, or to York Bay to see the penguins. Islanders do drive to the camp once the land has dried out thoroughly, but even then they need to know the terrain exceptionally well and even so still often get bogged down never to reach their fishing destination. By now a few more miles of surfaced road will doubtless have been added, including a road to the temporary airstrip.

In Stanley I never ceased to be surprised at how often people would hop into their Land Rovers to make a journey of only a few hundred yards. Very few people walked, and as Stan would remark, 'they take on the shape of their Land

5. Beaver float plane (FIGAS).

Rovers after a while.' When we were still newcomers, I used to get fed up with Land Rovers drawing up beside me and a voice saying 'Want a lift?' After a while they realised that *Madame, la Col. Sec.* preferred to walk. Thereafter, they just whizzed past, but by then there were occasions when I would have welcomed a lift as I lugged a heavy shopping basket along the sea wall for the three-quarters of a mile from the West Store to Sulivan House.

Behind Stanley lie the peat bogs and in summer, people spend long hours cutting their peat, rickling it and finally bringing it home to store in their sheds. Luckily, the days are

6. The road to Stanley from Sulivan House.

long during the southern summer. The sun rises at about 3.00 or 4.00 in the morning and darkness does not fall until about 11 o'clock at night, thus giving ample time to accomplish all their jobs before the onset of the Antarctic winter.

The fuel officer allocates each household a peatbog of about 150 yards; people try to get it cut in November, thereby giving the peat two or three months to dry out thoroughly before bringing it home in January or February by lorry or in a trailer attached to a Land Rover. Peat cutting is hard work; the sods are cumbersome and heavy when wet and skill is needed to throw them off the shovel. They are then rickled and left in piles to dry, which causes them to shrink considerably. They are left, rickled, for several months according to weather conditions and at an opportune moment, are brought back to the peat sheds where they are dumped in large piles.

Then begins the arduous task of chucking them in to form a solid wall. One is always working in arrears to give more time for the peat to dry out thoroughly; otherwise, you will not have the cheerful glow desired and your Rayburn will only smoke. Dampish peat sods are useful for banking, however, to keep the fire from burning away too quickly and keep it in at night. Peat mould is also useful for this purpose. We usually had eight or nine lorry loads of peat delivered for a year's supply, which in all cost about £45 for cutting and transport. In addition, in bad weather, we had oil fired central heating as well as electric heaters. Three forms of heat on the go at the same time were expensive, particularly as, after our years in West Africa, our central heating was on throughout the day, winter and summer alike.

The Agricultural Department, which has its stables not far from Sulivan House, kept a number of horses. Falkland Islands horses have ugly faces and a girth approaching that of a carthorse. They used to browse in the field beyond, but whenever an opportunity presented itself in the shape of an open gate they would make a beeline for what must have been greener grass down by the sea wall and would trot past like naughty children playing truant. The government bull was also put out to grass in the field adjoining Dolphin Cottage and it used to annoy the Heathman family by peering through their kitchen window, which they found particularly irritating when it took to bellowing, in either hope or frustration, as it followed Stan's cow around. This bull was held in some ridicule by Stanley knowalls because he was still very stunted at a stage when further growth seemed unlikely, rendering his potency in doubt and it was reckoned that the government had bought a pup. Before we left, however, he had grown to a more normal size and gave promise of being able to fulfil his duties adequately.

A hundred yards or so behind Sulivan House is the racecourse where Fitzgerald planted his flag and on which the hijacked plane later landed. Since then, obstructions have been placed at intervals along the length of the course to deter any further aerial invasion and are only removed for race meetings, which are held annually over the Christmas period. These meetings are not occasions for dressing up – gumboots, headscarves and anoraks being the order of the day – as the racecourse is a notoriously windy spot, even in the shelter of the grandstand. Races were well attended even when it snowed and the bars did a roaring trade. It was not unusual to be accosted on these occasions by reeling characters from the camp, in back-slapping mood regardless of the hierarchy! In addition to the usual plates and cups, there were handsome money prizes and expensive donations from the Falkland Islands Company; the competition was fierce. The race meetings always ended with a tug of war, with 3 teams competing from Stanley, the Marines from Moody Brook and the camp. The Marines usually left the field looking shamefaced after conceding annual victory to the mutton eaters.

Prior to my departure for the Falkland Islands, I had been told that Sulivan House was a charming residence and in fact, with the sun pouring in through the large windows facing the harbour and the prevailing westerly winds blowing, it was delightful, with magnificent views from every room, but it had its drawbacks when the wind blew to the south, which often entailed being snowed on in the loo, or to the southeast, when the kitchen grew icy and the Rayburn refused to draw, or to the north when it brought driving rain, which invariably penetrated all the cracks and joints of the windows along the front of the house resulting in pools of water. This was a penalty one had to accept as all the houses were sensibly oriented towards the north to catch the maximum amount of sun.

Fortunately, it was a spacious house and we were able to move from room to room according to the wind direction, so roomy, in fact, that I was able to relegate a very cold bedroom – anyone who slept there would have frozen to death anyway – into a shoe room. What luxury! Another bedroom housed my chemist shop. Stores in Stanley had very limited supplies of medicines and cosmetics and, as there was no chemist, a large number of items one would normally buy over the counter were unobtainable locally, even from the hospital, which frequently ran out of remedies due to postal and shipping delays and red tape at the other end. It was wise to keep a stock in hand and I got over the difficulty by ordering an 18-month supply at a time from Boots export department in Britain. On one occasion when I borrowed Mrs Heathman's bicycle to go to town she asked me to get her some Alka Seltzer to help relieve her rheumatism. I searched high and low, but every shop was out of it as it was near the festive season.

When we were first there I used to wake up at regular intervals and swear I could hear heavy-footed animals tramping round the house. It was, of course, only the wind. During storms the wooden panelling would creak like an old sailing ship and upstairs in bed one could literally feel the house swaying in the wind. Once, during a period of extensive gale force winds, we had to summon the Harbour Master's Department to lower our flagpole. Flags in Stanley had a very limited life and had to be renewed several times a year. When Mr Lewis arrived as Governor he asked for a bigger and better flag than had previously been in use – indeed the size which regulations prescribed, but soon realised his error when the larger flag was found to be in shreds in no time.

Like most houses in the Falkland Islands, our front door had the added protection of a glassed-in porch, but outside ours a headless angel stood guard, a relic of one of the many wrecks around those shores. Along the front of the house was the usual protective conservatory in which geraniums and fuchsias grew in tropical profusion throughout the year, throwing a magnificent splash of exotic colour against the white paintwork. The temperature there often climbed to 90° and I spent many an hour basking among the flowers, having transformed the conservatory into a sun room with the addition of comfortable chairs, a table, two casement windows, which I had persuaded the PWD to instal, and a fishnet over the door to keep the blowflies out in warm weather. When the sun shone I was back in Africa. Both sitting room and dining room, which looked onto the conservatory, were pleasantly comfortable with their grey velvet curtains and deep red carpeting, a souvenir of the visit by the Duke of Edinburgh some 15 years earlier. After the visit the royal carpet was cut up and distributed round various government houses.

The study was next to the sitting room and as the interior walls were mostly made of plywood I could hold a conversation with John through them. Two telephones, one a hot line to Government House, graced the heavy desk there. Both had old-fashioned handles which had to be wound furiously in order to gain the attention of the exchange, as well as to indicate to the exchange that a call had been completed. Stanley was such a small place that most of one's movements were known; this went for everybody, so if you were unable to obtain an answer from someone's house the girl on duty at the exchange could usually tell you where you would be likely to make successful contact.

The kitchen quarters, which looked onto the peat shed at the back of the house, consisted of a large kitchen, pantry and scullery; these had obviously been intended for palmier days when skivvies abounded to answer the bell indicators above the kitchen door. Even the bathroom had a bellpush and when I was feeling particularly bloody-minded or in a playful mood I used to ring it imperiously, especially if I knew that John happened to be nearby. On one occasion when the air attaché from the British embassy in Buenos Aires was visiting us and noticed me leaping up and down from the dinner table, he asked me why I didn't ring the bell. I looked at him in disgust and said, 'because there's no bugger to answer it'.

A large double-ovened Rayburn took up most of one wall in the kitchen, but due to some quirk only one oven functioned; whereas the right-hand side frequently went off the clock if the wind blew in a certain direction, resulting in a gurgling tank which had to have the hot water run off to prevent it from going brown with rust. Stan used to tell an amusing story about how, when Rayburns were first introduced to the colony, one camper tore the oven door off its hinges and flung it outside when it overheated. All Rayburns have a rail along the front and this is where Falkland Islanders, and anyone else for that matter, take up their favourite stance of leaning back against the rail to toast themselves.

Next to the Rayburn was a peat box and innumerable peat buckets made from oil drums. A supply was brought in three or four times a day. The Rayburn supplied all the hot water and must therefore be kept burning day and night. Those oil drums had various uses besides being peat holders; the large ones served as water butts and others as refuse and ash containers. Goose feathers must not be omitted from the Rayburn scene as no kitchen was ever without them, nor of course the inevitable peat gloves to handle hot oven door handles and peat sods, the chemicals of which made one's hands dry and discoloured. When I first saw a goose feather on the kitchen floor I thought it was a plaything for the cat, but I soon came to realise and appreciate its usefulness, far more effective than any ordinary brush. In fact, in my loads I packed enough to supply my needs for several years. I was fortunate that, in addition to the Rayburn, which restricts the method of cooking, Sulivan House had an ancient electric cooker. Its grill pan was missing and after much explanation and trial and error the PWD managed to make one by soldering bits and pieces to the sides of a baking tin and then adding a handle. The first attempt produced too short a handle, but a second was successful and I had a usable grill pan. I was able to make toast at last!

When we arrived at Sulivan House, oil-fired central heating had just been installed replacing the peat-fired system, but all the old-fashioned iron fireplaces had been left intact. On my instructions these were all boarded up except for the large grate in the sitting room. Those skivvies must have worked very hard, for each of the four bedrooms had a fireplace and one can imagine the endless trail of peat buckets being ferried up and down stairs by panting wenches. The main reason for boarding up the fireplaces was that at least 50 per cent of the benefit of the central heating was disappearing up the eight open fireplaces in the house, and with oil at £30 a delivery, later to go up to nearly £50, this was hardly economic, but we did retain the sitting-room fire. It had an attractive arched, handmade stone surround, of which only three others existed in Stanley, the design of which enhanced the glow from the peat fire. It had a large open grate through which the peat dust fell to pile up in a grey mound. A different approach was needed to bank this fire to keep it going until the next morning. When the fire had burned low, peat sods were first laid flat and then grey dust piled on top until the sods were well covered, just allowing a meagre trickle of smoke to emerge, and so it smouldered away slowly during the night, till it was riddled the next morning whereupon the fire would burst into flame again. In our household I was the kitchen Rayburn expert, while John specialised in the sitting-room fire.

The two main bedrooms overlooked the harbour, as did the tiny room in between. This I turned into a hide for watching the seabirds which nested on the hulk opposite. Sulivan House had at one time belonged to Packe Brothers and the *Jhelum* had been their trading hulk. She was a small, picturesque vessel with a fine curving bow and still retained some vestiges of her original working gear, such as the capstan. As she was the last hulk which could be approached by a jetty, it provided a popular tourist attraction, but I fear not for much longer as the jetty is decaying and the hulk is gradually losing her battle with the wind and tide. On one occasion the Harbourmaster broadcast an invitation for those interested to make bids for acquiring wrecks and I seriously thought of bidding for the *Jhelum*. There was something romantic about the idea of owning a piece of history, but the thought of the difficulties that might arise from simultaneous ownership of a precarious jetty dissuaded me. One night when the *Philomel* caught fire in harbour in mysterious circumstances, I feared that my hulk might go up in flames too because once the blaze had been brought under control the *Philomel* was towed to and tied up alongside the *Jhelum*. I was awakened at midnight by the glow of the blazing ship lighting up the bedroom. This time the fire had too much of a hold and fearing for the safety of the hulk and houses nearby, had the wind got up, the burning ship was towed over to Fairy Cove opposite Sulivan House on the other side of the harbour, to burn itself out.

7. The *Jhelum* on the jetty outside Sulivan House.

The most irritating feature of Sulivan House was undoubtedly the bathroom as the pipes were so furred up that it took an eternity for the water to force its way up from the kitchen and along the pipe system to trickle out into the bath in a slow, thin brown stream. It was useless for John to try to have a bath first thing in the morning as he would never have reached his office in time and in the evening we often used to turn the tap on and then go out for a walk. The bath would be ready 40 minutes later and we were able to enjoy our walk without any fear of it overflowing. Some of the piping was renewed at the end of our first year and for a while we were able to enjoy morning baths, but long before we left the colony the flow was down to a trickle again.

Sulivan House carried a few interesting mementoes of its past. The paddock behind the house had at one time been a formal flower garden and the shapes of the beds were still visible. Occasionally, a stray flower would appear to confront a startled cow. An old boiler house near the kitchen door must at one time have been a stable, for there was a mounting block outside and set in the garden wall further along were several iron rings for tethering horses. A modern relic, near the front gate, was our own white Belisha beacon. This was controlled by a switch inside the front porch and, when lit, was a sign that we were entertaining or at home to visitors.

Because of the weather one is more tied to a house in the Falkland Islands than in most countries and I must admit that I became very attached to my island home; I expect a little bit of me will always be there in the conservatory among the geraniums or sitting in the sun in the doorway looking out towards the sea wall. I discovered that various Colonial Secretaries' wives tend to be remembered for their individual idiosyncracies. For example, there was one who always wore a gown, another who died, an eccentric who wore gumboots to all functions, including Government House cocktail parties and yet another who baked toffee apples to distraction. I expect to be remembered for my propensity for following the sun.

It is human nature, fortunately, to remember the more agreeable aspects of a particular place rather than its discomforts and lack of amenities, for the memory of the biting, numbing wind to fade and to be replaced by a cloudless blue sky and shimmering sea, on one of those rare, calm summer day when everything was bathed in a pure crystal light and the shouts of horsemen rounding up sheep could be heard from across the harbour as if they were in a nearby field; to forget the demands of the Rayburn, to which one had to make a beeline on entering the house, clad in evening finery or not, in order to feed the brute, and to recall instead its comforting warmth as one leaned, in typical Falkland Island fashion, against its rail; to forget about bringing in the washing in the teeth of an icy gale-force wind, avoiding being knocked senseless by the gate *en route*, and to recall instead the fresh smell of wind-dried clothes; to forget about the difficulties of cooking and contrast it instead with being able to pick sun-warmed tomatoes from the greenhouse; to forget the days of sudden, violent squalls and flurries of hail, sleet and snow in midsummer, the periods when the wind went round to the south and the Rayburn refused to draw and one scuttled in and out of an Antarctic kitchen, and to remember instead the sun streaming through the large windows to bathe the house in a soft, golden glow, or walking over the tussac to the outcrop of sun-warmed rocks behind the racecourse; for the memory to fade of the days when the inner harbour was whipped to a frenzy of white horses and blankets of blown spray and to remember instead a prevailing westerly wind, light and fresh from the hills beyond, or a calm night when the wind had dropped completely and the lights along the sea wall were reflected on a flat, calm sea; to appreciate in retrospect the days when one had time to stand and stare on your way along the sea wall towards town.

On such days it was wise to drop everything in order to take advantage of the comparative warmth andpeace, as it was a certainty it would not last long and that a few hours later the wind would spring up from nowhere and with the wind the temperature would immediately drop. In the Falkland Islands the wind is said to blow at gale force one day in five and one must admit, whatever one says about the landscape, that the climate was anything but monotonous. In a masochistic way I almost miss the cold, tingling blast of fresh air coming straight from the southern icecaps and the need to pit one's energy and resources against the elements.

Chapter 7
The Silly Season

After we had been in the colony for two months Sir Cosmo and Lady Haskard, with their son Julian, went on leave and John took over as Acting Governor and High Commissioner. We saw them off on RMS *Darwin* at the Public jetty which was lined by the Marines in honour of their departure. The Governor had insisted that it was not to be a formal occasion and informality was indeed its hallmark. The Marines were caught off guard for once as they lounged at ease awaiting the arrival of the Government House taxi. In its place a Land Rover rolled up, thereby causing a moment of military confusion. The taxi had broken down in the Government House driveway and since there were no spare parts available and *Darwin* was about to go into dry dock, the vehicle was off the road until the Governor's return from leave.

The Falkland Islands flag with its silly sheep in the centre now flapped from our flagpole from early morning until sunset. This flag used to display a handsome dolphin, which I would have thought more appropriate even though the colony's resources do rely on the sheep's back. During this period we settled in and got the feel of the place. Memories of mammoth cooking sessions and brewing jugs of rum punch for cocktail parties at Sulivan House spring to mind, while John commuted between Government House and the Secretariat, combining the two jobs of Governor and Col. Sec. Otherwise, Stanley was quiet, as the colony had closed down for the winter and drawn into its island fastness.

No ships called, not even the *Darwin,* which had gone into drydock in Montevideo for an extended period. We were without mail for some time until the MV *Forrest* made a trip to Punta Arenas in Chile to collect timber and much needed mail. Adrian Monk, who managed the Port San Carlos farm on East Falkland, agreed to act as master for the voyage because Jack Sollis, ordinarily the master, preferred not to sail the ship in international waters. I can remember this period as one of terrific winds but bright sunshine. This combination had the effect of turning one's face a dark shade of mahogany, making an odd contrast with the rest of one's body which, being well covered with clothing, remained lily white.

The wind, which is reported to reach gale force one day in five, blows to a greater or lesser degree every day. Frequently there would often be no flying for periods of up to a week until the gale had spent itself. Sometimes it would be dangerous, or even impossible, to attempt to walk along the sea wall and could be such a struggle along the road to town that it was wiser to follow a circuitous route through the fields and over the stiles behind Government House to the football field. But, depending on the direction of the wind, even that could be difficult and I have often dodged up one Government House drive and down another to secure the protection of the high hedges and to avoid being drenched by sea spray. On one occasion I deposited a precious bottle of whisky at the Secretariat rather than risk carrying it home in such hazardous wind conditions. In such winds umbrellas are useless and the local people certainly never use them; and I very much doubt if they even own any. Ours made a useless journey from Europe to the South Atlantic and back. The one and only time I suggested to Stan that perhaps I should take my umbrella in case of rain, he laughed himself silly; umbrellas were obviously a big joke, and I noticed that my reaction two years later when Mrs Lewis sent for hers was somewhat similar to Stan's.

During this period an Agricultural Team arrived to write a much needed report on the colony's main industry and to recommend, it was hoped, ways of improving it. It was a magnificent team consisting of three Welshmen, one Irishman and one Scot. It did a first-class job, although the eventual report was unpopular with farm managers who did not care to face some of the unpalatable facts included in it. Although based in Stanley, the members of the team spent much of their time commuting to and from camp.

It was fortunate that the colony had available a house large enough to accommodate the team, while a local woman was found who, for a very reasonable consideration, was prepared to keep house for them. As their assignment involved them in constant inter-island travel, such an arrangement was essential as there was no hotel able to house them. These arrangements assisted the development of a team spirit.

On their return from camp they usually had amusing experiences to relate of the hazards of the 'two-nighter' – the drinking-cum-dancing marathon in which campers indulged whenever there was an event worthy of celebration; or of avoiding the attentions of certain amorously inclined women; or of farmers' wives vying with each other over the hour at which they got up to milk the cow and their husbands' subsequent annoyance at the early retiral of the womenfolk, in anticipation of winning the next round; of being wakened by blazing sunlight at three in the morning (camp time is an hour ahead of Stanley in summer) and there being no curtains to cut out the light being obliged to get dressed and go fishing. There were more tales of baths and 'buggers to float', of sick cows and cats, and the graphic account of a droving expedition related by Bill Williams, the laboratory technician.

Bill had joined Richard Cockwell, the manager of Fox Bay East, and his shepherds, in droving sheep to collect livestock blood samples for his laboratory tests. The campers had, of course, expected Bill to fall off his mount, but he did not give them that pleasure and spent several sore and weary days in the saddle, even managing to adapt to the gaucho-like sideways method of riding prevalent in the islands. They spent their nights in primitive huts where they would tumble, fully clad, into bunks supplied with sheepskins. The assortment of engraved cutlery from wrecked ships remained unused, as they ate roughly, using the working knives from their belts to slice off hunks of mutton. Bill had to follow suit or starve.

I had but one fault to find with the agricultural team. As the majority of them were Welsh, they were apt to foregather at a certain witching hour to indulge in their favourite pastime, the Welsh being compulsive singers as are canaries!

The colony has had its fair share of agricultural reports. In the early 1920s, a New Zealander called Munro spent a considerable amount of time there and wrote a useful report, but the farming community failed to implement his recommendations. In the mid-1930s, Davis wrote his report on grasslands, but it had the misfortune to be published just before the outbreak of the Second World War, so was more handicapped than is usual with reports. While it is true that one or two of the establishments engaged in farming in the colony had struck out on some of the lines recommended by Munro, there had been no concerted attempt by the farming community as a whole to put his recommendations into effect, in particular as regards improving quality through selective breeding. So far as the Davis report on on grasslands was concerned the situation was somewhat similar. Some farms had carried out experiments along the lines suggested by Davis but, by and large, little had been done. The effective situation was that during this century the sheep population of the colony had declined from over 800,000 to over 600,000. There was evidence to show that while the Falkland Islands wool retained its unique quality, a quality for which no firm explanation is available, the grasslands continued to deteriorate. It was against this background and in an economic climate inimical to wool prices that the Davies team had to work.

This agricultural team, which visited the colony under the auspices of the British Ministry Overseas Development aid programme, had all the specialists it needed for the task assigned to it, including backup laboratory facilities. The team was composed of agronomists, experts on sheep and cattle, a veterinary surgeon and a laboratory technician. It was clearly hoped that a high-powered team of this kind would carry weight with the colony's farming community and that its recommendations would materially contribute to the colony's future economic welfare. While I am sure that the names, characters and personal foibles of the team members will linger in the islands' folk memory for a long time, it did seem at the time we left, that the fate of their report, overlong in the printing in Britain, through no fault of the team, was likely to suffer a similar fate as those of its predecessors Munro and Davis.

Some islanders believe that the decision of an earlier Governor to wind up the government's demonstration farm during a period of financial stringency, around the time of the slump, was disastrous and a false economy for a community so dependent on sheep. The 1971 report contains a strong recommendation to set up a demonstration farm with direct links to research establishments in Britain. It also recommends forging links with internationally-manned agricultural research stations in Argentina. The team visited some of these stations at the end of their time in the islands, a comprehensive if short itinery arranged courtesy of the Royal Navy, whose good ship performed one of her many Fairy Godmother acts by lifting the team across to the mainland when other transport was unavailable. Close family links already exist between Patagonia and Islands families. Provided the political climate remains settled, extending these links would definitely benefit the two sets of farming communities. Already some closer contacts are beginning to be made.

I shall not attempt to describe in any detail all the recommendations in the Davies Report. This lengthy document, with many technical appendices, sets out a blueprint for the future of the colony's agriculture, which, it states firmly, must remain based on sheep. The long-term nature of most of the recommendations is stressed, as is their limited use in a world where economic priorities and climates change so rapidly. For the government and the industry the main problem is finance. In recent years the colony's government has made unremitting efforts to contain the cost of its recurrent services while keeping its new capital commitments to a necessary frugal minimum.

Capital needs are easy to identify. A new electricity generating plant, fortunately now being constructed, was needed to replace a plant more than twenty years old and second-hand when originally purchased and installed. This project receives finance from British aid funds. A certain amount of capital will be needed to effect reforms on the medical and educational services and some infrastructure is obviously needed for tourism. To purchase land for a government demonstration farm, to equip and staff it will be expensive. There will be a need to spend money on the colony's internal transport system. While all these are probably necessary, they will not all contribute to improving the quality of life; but rather to maintaining current standards. The recent slight improvement in wool prices has evidently given the farmers, who dominate the government's councils, more confidence in the future, but there are formidable problems ahead.

Falkland Islanders have so far managed to muddle through, but in the world of the mid-1970s muddling through was not a solution to be recommended. Medium- and long-term planning is vital, but is foreign to the islanders' temperament. The Davies Report has stimulated and will continue to stimulate thought on the main industry's problems, but it is not, nor was it claimed by its authors to be, a final solution.

The Governor, Sir Cosmo Haskard, returned in October to be followed by Lady Haskard in November. She arrived just in time to participate in the Remembrance Day parade on 11 November and to organise the annual activities of the Red Cross. Lady H. was a woman of tremendous energy and enthusiasm for the task in hand – whether that was feeding hens, chasing geese, acting as *major-domo* in the kitchen or organising committees and shows. As Stan would say in an admiring tone, 'The lady makes a good navvy boss.'

With the arrival of the RRS *John Biscoe*, the first of the British Antarctic Survey ships, the season was now upon us. After the quiet of the winter this resurrection came as a surprise, as did the period of intense shipping activity in and out of Stanley harbour. The liveliness of the islands contrasted strangely with the long period of hibernation when they withdrew behind cloaks of peat smoke and blown spume, withdrawing into the customary isolation enforced by the elements, such solitude being taken for granted. The sudden resuscitation came almost as a shock, as instead of a gentle awakening from winter sleep the islanders were jolted wide awake by buzzing helicopters, booming naval gun salutes, strident ships' sirens, noisy derricks, the shuttling of small craft to and from all the jetties of Stanley, strange voices and faces in the streets and shops where there was a roaring trade selling cameras and watches to bearded FIDS, and the visual impact of the gay, scarlet naval and BAS ships against the sombre grey end-of-winter backdrop.

Stanley's maidens (and matrons let it be whispered) also perked up and parties galore were held both aboard and ashore, with a preponderance of gallant males in attendance. The ratio of men to women was always greater in the islands, but with the numbers swollen by the navy and BAS the female of the species blossomed like a desert rose. The formal drawing room at Government House, where such functions were held, was bursting at the seams. Guests were seen through a haze of cigarette smoke and blue uniform, while Queen Victoria looked down frostily upon the festivities.

At parties, Falkland Islanders behaved as if strict segregation of the sexes was *de rigueur*, the men congregating in small groups to talk shop while the women discussed domestic matters. But for the white faces one would have thought oneself in a small town in West Africa where a similar segregation of the sexes was usual at social functions. On these occasions during the season, the men were happy to leave a clear field to the seafarers and retire, reasonably well lubricated, glass in hand and sweating profusely, clad as they usually were in thick suits and waistcoats, mopping their brows at the unaccustomed heat generated by so many bodies in close proximity, to the freshness of the conservatory, ablaze with colourful flowers and pot plants.

The Government House cat, a temperamental Siamese, adored these gatherings and would view them with a proprietary air from the back of an armchair, from which it made mad darts between guests' legs. Government House entertained lavishly and during the season, when guests were many and hotels non-existent until the Upland Goose got under way, it used to take on the aspect of a hotel with house parties overflowing into the billiard room where camp beds were set up.

Shortly after our arrival in the colony we made a discovery regarding the rigid customs pertaining to cocktail parties at Government House, which were held from 6.45 to 8.00 p.m. Guests would turn up some ten minutes before the appointed hour and queue along the corridor leading to the drawing room as if under starter's orders, in the strictest order of seniority, till the butler-cum-chauffeur gave the starting signal, and black were the looks if anyone did not know his place. We were apparently expected to be first in the queue, but since we disliked this form of regimentation we would arrive a few minutes later than the appointed time (except on special occasions where to be late would have been discourteous to a distinguished guest) and were eventually able to break the hierarchical custom.

Very large quantities of liquor were consumed at these gatherings, Falkland Islanders being good topers at all times, no doubt getting some of their taxes back in kind. I remember Mr Lewis's surprise at the speed at which his liquor ration disappeared. He had underestimated his guests' capacity by several months.

At 8.00 p.m. it was customary for the Colonial Secretary and his wife to remind the Governor that it was 'time, gentlemen, please' and to lead the way out, thus giving the signal to the other guests to queue up to thank and say goodnight to their host and hostess. When distinguished visitors were present we were kept very busy introducing them to leading personalities of the local and expatriate communities, ensuring that they were filled in on local matters, and steering them away from limpets and awkward customers.

Dinner parties were normally formal black tie occasions, providing the women with an opportunity to climb out of their practical garments and become gaudy butterflies for a few hours in a relaxed, unhurried atmosphere of gracious living, the dark mahogany dinner table agleam with silver candelabra and cream lace napery, and brilliant flower table decorations garnered from the conservatory, the room lit by the soft glow of candles and a blazing peat fire. As always at Government House, His Excellency is served first and at the end of the meal everyone stands at his invitation to drink the loyal toast. After a discreet interval the Governor's wife would go through the motions of 'catching the eye' of the first lady on the Governor's right to sweep us off to powder our noses, thence to the formal drawing room for coffee to await the arrival of the gentlemen, suffused with food, port and cigars, whereupon everyone would stand until the Governor was seated.

Two balls a year, the New Year's Ball and the Queen's Birthday Ball, were held at Government House when annual chaos and draughts ensued, with the removal of carpets, doorways and furniture to make room for the hundred or more selected guests who had been invited to dance to records in the drawing room. Printed programmes were strictly adhered to and in Governor Haskard's time these would feature numerous Circassian Circles and Eightsome Reels, but with the arrival of Mr Lewis more modern dances, in keeping with the new Governor's more 'with-it' gear, were introduced. In Governor Haskard's time the balls were usually jolly, fairly informal evenings, with the emphasis on food at midnight, whereas Mr Lewis's approach was more formal with navy personnel from Moody Brook filling the role of press photographer to take horrid pictures of us all cavorting. Unused to such formality, the islanders at the Queen's Birthday Ball were apt to get under the Governor's feet when he and his wife entered the room to take up their stance beneath the august photographic presence of Queen Victoria and continued to chatter until the Colonial Secretary was obliged to call for silence for His Excellency.

Apart from entertaining at home the Governor and his wife would make periodic visits to camp, usually by Beaver, although some Governors, Haskard from choice and others from necessity went on horseback along the old tracks, at one time the only means of communication between settlements.

More weddings would be held during the season than at other times of the year and this frequently entailed putting in an appearance and providing a wedding present. Fortunately, 'his and her' towels were in vogue in the Newest Store (as the FIC advertisements on The Box grandiosely called it). Weddings were always grand affairs with a reception in the Town Hall, followed later by a dance to which most of Stanley would be invited. The invitation was usually extended to any campers who happened to be in town and the Beaver flight schedules would be full for days. When one thinks of the planning and effort involved in ordering the wedding dress and bridesmaids' clothes from Britain and, ensuring their arrival in time by the infrequent voyages of the MV *AES*, it is staggering that they usually did turn up. Once in a while local shops would be frantically raided for remnants and dresses would be run up at the last moment by René Rowlands.

Islanders and expatriates alike use mail order catalogues, but, by the time the parcel arrives by *AES*, one has frequently forgotten what was ordered or even that anything was ordered at all as there could be a time lapse of six months or more.

A few months after our arrival in Stanley, Stan's daughter Jenny married into the police force, which did her proud with an archway of batons and a guard of honour. Everything for that wedding had been ordered from Britain, the white wedding dress and veil, yellow dresses for the bridesmaids, pale blue ensemble and hat for the mother of the bride, and Stan, in a brand new suit, had, in honour of the occasion, taken his teeth out of the drawer.

***

John sailed on the *John Biscoe* for South Georgia from where the administrator and other staff were to be evacuated as the administration of the dependency was to be taken over by the BAS. A number of wives had been living in South Georgia so on this occasion women did travel on a BAS ship, thus breaching Sir Vivian Fuchs's stringent policy – 'no women on my ships'. John found his visit to South Georgia extremely interesting and spent many hours on the ship's bridge watching seabirds and observing the crew going about their various duties.

On her way along the east coast, the *John Biscoe* dropped anchor off Prion Island in the Bay of Isles where some FIDS went ashore in one of the ship's Gemini rubber launches to spend an afternoon botanising among the rocks while others landed on the gently shelving shore to investigate the large penguin colony, whose inhabitants performed amazing alpine feats in an attempt to escape scientific scrutiny.

As they sailed on next morning hugging the coastline of South Georgia, the breathtaking panorama of successive glaciers – Lucas, Morris, Crean, named after a member of Scott's Antarctic expedition, Fortuna, König and the massive Neumayer – the contrasting muted shades of blue, green and brown against this stark white grandeur brought home the superb skill of the illustrator Edmund Wilson, Scott's friend and companion.

As the ship sailed into Cumberland Bay, the Nordenskjöld glacier and series of majestic snowy peaks beyond it, culminating in Mount Paget at 10,000 feet, formed a magnificent backdrop before the ship turned to starboard to enter King Edward Cove. The feeling of having arrived in Antarctica was complete, though strictly speaking South Georgia is not within the orbit of the peninsula; nonetheless, the white island has the look and feel of the south.

The station at King Edward Point, a huddle of low houses under the hill, is dominated by one building, Shackleton House, the size and opulence of which is incongruous in such a setting. Able to accommodate some 60 people in separate bedsitters, and with a large modern kitchen, the enormous windows of the dining room look directly onto the harbour, alive with elephant seal, and across the bay to a snowy landscape. As is so often the case when an empire is in decline, Shackleton House was finished in time to be abandoned, and it would have been but for the fact that the BAS, after prolonged negotiations with the government of the Falkland Islands and Dependencies, was taking over South Georgia as a permanent Antarctic scientific base and, at the same time, establishing the essential administrative presence there. It was because of this changeover that my husband made this trip.

John did not consider that King Edward Point had a great deal of character, but his visit was more than compensated by a walk he took to Grytviken along a stony beach, past tussac grass where giant grey elephant seals rested. The entire beach was littered with pieces of whalebone, in fact there was so much of it that he saw no point in taking a piece away as a souvenir, which he later regretted, but the spectacle at close quarters of elephant seal performing aquatic sports in the still deep water dispelled the ghosts.

With its ghosts of whalers and leviathans of the deep, Grytviken had a romantic atmosphere, yet when John visited

South Georgia, a few whale-catchers were still tied up at the quayside. The company which rented the station from the Colony Government still retained one maintenance engineer there, but knowing that the whaling industry from fixed shore bases was gone forever it was another incongruous touch to see the neatness of the repair work he continued to carry out on those catchers. From the photographs John took of them, the repairs could well have been done by a Norwegian shipyard. Nearby, with the winches still in place, was the flensing plan, the centre of activity in whaling days, with its heavy timber floor sloping slightly upwards from the water level. This was where the whale carcasses were hauled up for the hard work of flensing and stripping and where the blood flowed. The size of the platform and of the winches conveyed an impression of just how huge those creatures were. John never tired of visiting the plan to recreate in his imagination the activity of a vanished industry. The conservationists may have given whaling a bad name, but like any ghost town, Grytviken is still alive with memories.

Other places of interest to visit apart from the plan were the church, Norwegian in style and architecture, bearing the date 1921, and a rather unattractive Wild West type of cinema, its nondescript façade dated 1924. The empty manager's house, with its portrait of King Haakon and dining table set ready for guests, had a fairytale feel. Neglect and the accumulated weight of snow on the roofs had caused some of the oil tanks and stores to collapse inwards, but even in the humdrum stores, imagination could be given full rein. Equipment lay neatly in racks, numbered, itemised and described. There was hemp rope, nylon rope, sailing gear, spares for the workshop to the value of hundreds of thousands of pounds, yet all completely worthless, since it was not to anybody's advantage to take it away. The workshops were well kept and capable of carrying out major repairs provided the electrical plant for the station was reactivated. Now that the whalers have departed the elephant seals have taken over Grytviken, along alleyways, on slipways, on doorsteps, on paths, on the plan itself (no ghosts troubled them), on piles of rusting pan or girders – they are everywhere. Their agility on land was surprising in view of their bulk and they could negotiate a pile of dangerous looking debris with very little effort and at great speed, but usually they stood their ground, rearing up ferociously and defeating you with their fetid breath.

Continuing his tour of exploration, John found the small cemetery just beyond the whaling station; it contained, among others, the simple grave of Ernest Shackleton. A white wooden fence surrounded the tidily kept cemetery but seals, particularly baby seals, are no respecter of fences or people, so the fences are constantly being broken down and seals found sleeping among the graves. However, I am sure that the great explorers and those others who lie at rest in the remoteness of that South Georgian cemetery would have no objection and indeed would even welcome the companionship of the seal pups with their melting liquid eyes and attractive puppy fat. John brought back a large number of photographs of South Georgia, but I am sure that none of them can convey the sense of romantic solitude and of the vanity of man's effort in the south as a visit to this deserted spot.

The young scientists of the British Antarctic Survey spend a season, sometimes two, in South Georgia where, compared with their colleagues on bases further south, they are in clover. The Base Leader, Ricky Chinn, spends part of the year there and the rest in Britain. Russian ships call at King Edward Point, as do cruise ships, while the arrival of an Argentine vessel can cause complications. The base leader had the virtue of not flapping unnecessarily and the government in Stanley could be sure that everything was being handled in a sensible and level-headed manner. To his credit, Ricky kept us supplied, though not at all to excess, with reindeer meat. The herd on South Georgia, originally a dozen, has now increased to 4000 and some culling is necessary. Similar to venison, though less rich and therefore in our opinion superior to it, reindeer meat is for gourmets, but being faced with a whole quarter on the first occasion put a strain on my recipe books.

***

The Remembrance Day parade John missed was, like all ceremonies of its kind, very impressive, made more so by the presence of the detachment of Marines and sailors of the Hovercraft Unit, not to mention the contingent of the Falkland Islands Defence Force, the Boys' Brigade and the Girls' Brigade, and not least of all, the Governor, resplendent in plumes and magnificent in full regalia, his uniform of fine dark blue broadcloth with a wide red stripe down the trouser seam, the colourful sash of the Order of St Michael and St George, and medals and aiguilletes of silver. Sir Cosmo was tall and carried his uniform well, although I believe he found it so uncomfortable that he always disappeared quickly as soon as a ceremony was over to change.

There was unfortunately no Marine bugler, so the broadcasting unit played a tape: a landline linked it to the signal battery on Victory Green, which enabled it to relay by telephone to the waiting saluting team the word of command to fire. One year, I was told, there was a hitch and contact was not made, so there was no salute fired on that occasion. It was traditional, after the parades were over, for the Governor and the Colonial Secretary to repair to the FIDF Club, there to take part in a toast, the cost of which was one of the Governor's and

Colonial Secretary's privileges to bear. Two other annual parades were held during the year, one on 8 December to commemorate the naval Battle of the Falkland Islands, the other in celebration of Her Majesty's Birthday held in the colony in April due to the general inclement nature of the weather in the more usual month of June.

Parades were usually cold, windy occasions. On Remembrance Sundays a cold wind would funnel up the steps leading to the Cross of Sacrifice at the eastern extremity of the town, where we would sway in its blast. Wreaths had to be anchored with heavy weights. Another parade was held on 8 December to commemorate the naval battle of the Falklands and the defeat of the German Admiral Graf von Spee by the British Admiral Sturdee who sallied forth, under difficulties, from Port William to tackle and annihilate with the broadsides of the battle cruisers *Invincible* and *Implacable* the German fleet that had recently been victorious at Coronel. A Falkland Islands family played its part in this battle when a female servant ran to tell her mistress, the farm manager's wife, that she had sighted many ships passing in the colony's waters – it was the German battle fleet. The warning was passed on and because of it Sturdee's fleet was not taken by surprise as it otherwise might well have been. For the annual celebration of this battle a howling gale could normally be guaranteed, while for the Queen's Birthday parade on 21 April, the tail end of the silly season, snow would provide a reminder that winter was on the way.

At Mr Lewis's first parade as Governor, which was for the Queen's Birthday, it snowed and hailed alternately throughout the morning, giving rise to much toing and froing on the telephone between the Colonial Secretary at Sulivan House, Danny Borland at the meteorological office, the Marines at the Head of the Bay and the Governor at Government House, before it was eventually decided to go ahead with the outdoor arrangements for the parade which was held to the accompaniment of snow and driving hail. It was as well that this decision was taken because the bad weather arrangements for this parade had not been carried out for so long that they would probably have resulted in a fiasco. Penned at the front of the VIP enclosure, commonly known as the corral, getting the full blast of the elements, I was thankful when the ceremony was over to retire to Keith and Margaret Luxton's charming house where coffee and drinks were laid on to thaw out the frozen corpses, while the Governor and the Colonial Secretary did their usual honours at the Falkland Islands Defence Force Club.

Although alternative plans did exist for an indoor parade in the event of foul weather, in our three years there the weather always held out just sufficiently to allow the event to take place outdoors at the mercy of the winds. On this bitterly cold occasion the final decision rested with the Governor, who would be making his first appearance in gubernatorial rig. Whatever the weather the ceremonial parades were impressive, with the Governor resplendent in full uniform, the Marines likewise, the Hovercraft contingent vying with them in drill and elegance and the Falkland Islands Defence Force determined not to be outshone. To the uninitiated the Defence Force's performance always looked good, but I used to keep an eye on those among the spectators who were veterans of the Second World War, and when I saw them having a hard time suppressing their mirth I knew that all was not as well as it appeared. A move was afoot, instigated by the Colonial Secretary, to dispense with the raggle-taggle of the Boys' Brigade and Girls' Brigade, who, though valiantly turning up to these parades in all weathers, could be relied upon to drown, with their coughing and sneezing, the preceding cathedral service.

8. Marines on parade in Port Stanley with the Governor's vehicle (black taxi) in the rear.

Then came the arrival of the DAN boats which were still on charter at that time to the BAS while the completion of the much bigger and more modern vessel *Bransfield* was awaited, due to arrive the following year. The road to Government House seemed to be unusually full of pedestrians at this time as ships' masters, scientists and other bearded men of all ages to-ed and fro-ed to pay their respects. Governor Haskard was very conscious of his duties as High Commissioner for the British Antarctic Territory and was in the habit of inviting all new FIDS to his office before they set off down south for the first time.

Next to arrive was HMS *Endurance*, whose approach was heralded by buzzing helicopters and a 21-gun salute in honour of the Governor. During the season it was worth the effort to walk up the steep roads to Davis Street, high above the waterfront, to look over the magnificent harbour and through the Narrows to the waters of Port William beyond and enjoy the unusual sight of a full harbour of seven or eight ships. Throughout the season Stanley harbour was the scene of much frenetic shipping activity. Both naval and BAS ships were constantly in and out of port collecting mail, taking on water and supplies, or enjoying a brief stopover and relaxation on their way to Punta Arenas in southern Chile to collect and deposit VIPs, Marine detachments, research scientists and others of that ilk.

From time to time, Russian fishing vessels swelled the numbers in harbour to take on water and then sail away, their decks festooned with mutton carcasses. On one occasion, a Russian submarine, along with a Russian fishing research ship, asked permission to enter the harbour to refuel, and fieldglasses were trained on it from all quarters of Stanley. By the same token, a Russian sentry with a submachine gun warned off a boatload of curious BAS personnel trying to take a closer look at the submarine. By the time the season was drawing to a close and the ships had paid their last call to the the colony's port, the islanders almost looked forward to the coming winter period of undisturbed quiet.

The season heralded better weather, although it was not yet summer. Shipping had as yet penetrated only to the nearest southerly bases, as there was still too much ice down south. All naval and BAS ships going to the Antarctic are painted bright red, as are sledge ration boxes, this being the best colour to contrast with the black and white landscape; other colours would merge with the surroundings and the ships would be lost in a camouflaged world of indistinctness. When Signor Ajmone-Cat went south in his felucca-type yacht *San Giuseppe Due*, BAS personnel stationed in Stanley were worried about his vessel's black painted hull and persuaded him to carry some red paint on board, as the seas of the peninsula are treacherous. Although *Endurance* and BAS are constantly updating charts, uncharted rocks still present hazards, for example the holing of HMS *Endurance* soon after the accident to the *Lindblad Explorer*. BAS ships also take supplies to the bases and replacements for the FIDS who have been dug in there for the past year.

The first cruise ships also arrive at this time, but apart from the *Lindblad Explorer* they are too large to enter the inner harbour. The islands are usually on the cruise ships' itineraries, but an actual call there is at the captain's discretion and, because of poor weather conditions, they are often bypassed. The Red Cross headquarters, now called Emma Steen's Tearooms, were normally opened for the visit of a cruise ship and tea provided to swell Red Cross funds. Lady Haskard undertook the role of barker, standing outside the headquarters and encouraging tourists to enter and try the society's wares. The tourists, who were mostly American with a sprinkling of Scandinavians, Germans and South Americans, were impressed with the bonus of meeting a real live Governor's wife.

One party of tourists boldly walked up the drive to Government House and, through the large windows of the dining room, which look onto the drive and the side lawn with the flagstaff, took photographs of the Governor and his guests having lunch. That year the cakes in the Red Cross teahouse were out of tins as the year before, I was told, the members of the society had put in marathon baking sessions, only to find that, with adverse weather, cruise-ship calls were cancelled and they were left with the lot. However, the tourists seemed quite happy munching on what they fondly thought were homemade cakes and feeling very British drinking tea. Perhaps it was just as well that they were given Dundee cake, or whatever, for many islanders are in the habit of using mutton fat for baking and there is no disguising the taste of that; one might bite into what looked like a luscious chocolate cake only to have to repress a shudder on encountering an unmelted piece of mutton fat. That animal was certainly utilised in every conceivable way.

I took upon myself the job of translating 'toilet' into various languages, including American, as on being asked for the restroom, some Red Cross workers were directing tourists to seats in the tearoom. The Falkland Islands were not properly geared to tourism at that time; Land Rovers would turn up at the Public jetty to drive visitors round Stanley and to York Bay to see the penguin rookeries, but it was all done haphazardly. When John returned from South Georgia I handed him a lengthy minute based on the facts I had collected and the impressions formed during those two days of tourist-ship visits and recommended a number of measures to improve the situation. From this was born the idea of setting up a tourism committee. One of the results was the provision of public toilets. I had my uses!

Souvenirs were lacking apart from the usual plethora of nasty ashtrays made in Birmingham and other such trash. However, many tourists went on their way happily clutching penguin eggs to their bosoms. Since then the Guild of Spinners and Weavers has stepped up its efforts to produce local handicrafts, but one cannot help but feel that, with real drive and imagination, much more could be done. The Secretariat normally sends two of its young female staff out to the cruise ships to sell the *Falkland Islands Journal*, Cawkell's book on the

9. Penguins at York Bay.

colony and maps to the passengers. The Post Office also arranges for its staff to visit ships to sell the colony's popular stamp sets. Despite the lack of souvenirs, stores do a roaring trade. The Falkland Islands Company has been known to transact business on these occasions running into thousands of pounds, largely in cameras, watches, miniaturised binoculars and radios, as there is no tax on these items.

Another cruise ship which is now a regular visitor to the colony, not only to Stanley but to outlying islands such as New Island, West Point Island Island and Carcass Island, is the

Lindblad Explorer, which unlike the majority of cruise ships, has the advantage of being small enough to come into the inner harbour and tie up to the jetty. This ship is also more conservation oriented, carrying wildlife and other scientific lecturers and having a small but well-equipped laboratory-cum-lecture room aft. She has, however, had more than her fair share of misfortune. On her maiden voyage, while waiting to embark the majority of her passengers in Buenos Aires who were arriving by air, a fire in the galley, due to an electrical fault, caused the postponement of her first southerly cruise. Later, while riding out a snowstorm down south near Adelaide Island, she ran aground and was badly holed, her passengers receiving an unexpected and probably unwelcome bonus when put ashore to spend a few nights in the Antarctic in conditions they had not anticipated. This fine ship is now back in service, spending part of the year in Antarctic waters and the other part in the warmer seas around the Seychelles.

The SS *France*, on her first round-the-world cruise, also arrived while we were there with a full complement of widows and more to come. The colony was enjoying an unheard of spell of good weather with temperatures well up into the seventies and no wind to boot. Boatloads of elderly passengers were brought ashore preceded by ships stewards, who set up tables and chairs on the Public jetty, where there is normally a howling gale and one needs at least three layers of clothing to be able to remain there for any length of time. There they sat down to snacks while All-Stanley turned up to gape at this unusual spectacle.

When John walked along the sea wall after lunch that day, at the point where the wall dips below and out of sight of the road to Little Italy, he was electrified to hear, from the road above him, singing which sounded African and he was not far wrong, as at the point where the sea wall and road merge, he then met a party of Brazilians of almost pure African descent. In the bright Antarctic sunshine, these three men and two women were dancing and singing down the road in a way reminiscent of Lagos, or any other extrovert West African city.

When relations with Argentina improved, one cruise ship from that country, the *Argentina*, visited the colony. The British ambassador in Buenos Aires, Sir Michael Hadow, travelled in her, as did the minister in the Argentine foreign ministry, concerned with Falkland affairs, Señor Izaguirrez. The ambassador was making his second visit to the colony, but for the tourists aboard it was an unexpected visit. No announcement was made to the passengers that a visit to the colony was to be made until the ship was approaching the Narrows. No doubt, the news was intentionally withheld to avoid arousing patriotic feelings. The local story had it that so many of the passengers descended on the Falkland Islands Company that the staff lost track of the sales and much shoplifting took place. But how much truth there was in that, I do not know.

The question of flying national flags with its sovereignty implications was difficult, but on this occasion, with the ship moored in Port William, the visit happily passed off without incident. The problem did not arise when an Argentine ocean-going naval yacht, commanded by Commander Kelly, arrived in Stanley harbour because naval vessels do not fly courtesy flags. Both visits were in fact a great success with Falkland Islanders accepting invitations to social functions on board and trips round the harbour for children, in a spirit of good fellowship.

Chapter 8
Suprême de Volaille

By far the greatest attraction for tourists in the islands is and always will be the amazing variety of easily accessible wildlife. One had only to walk through Stanley and along the sea wall to see shags perched on the outlet pipe running into the harbour in front of the Secretariat, their heads swivelling above their white waistcoats, or night herons, hunched on a rock at low tide, or a pair of kelp geese muttering to each other as they pick and peck their way delicately among the green seaweed. Skuas and stinkers put on an aerial gliding exhibition as they sweep past you at eye level above the sea wall and a grey dolphin gull drops its mussel shell on the road right in front of you, while military starlings with their bright red breasts flitter in the grass and tiny yellow green siskins on the bushes. Stan once brought me a delicately made siskin's nest that had fallen to the ground. The nest was woven with bits of cotton, thread, horsehair, with dried grass and was beautifully and intricately constructed, and in it were the tiniest off-white eggs I have ever seen.

To see penguins streaking gracefully in and out of the pellucid water or stumbling clumsily over the rocks will compensate for the bumpy ride by Land Rover to York Bay or

10. Penguins on rocky outcrop.

Gipsy Cove. Five kinds of penguin can be seen in the Falklands, namely Rockhopper, Gentoo, Jackass, Macaroni and King, but beware of fleas and jabs at your ankles; it is wise to wear gumboots.

On one such excursion to the sand dunes at York Bay with Ted Gutteridge and his wife, we came across a small colony of Gentoos accompanied by a large King penguin which, unlike its smaller companions, stood his ground and eyed us disdainfully, looking very grand despite its moulting appearance. On the hillside above Gipsy Cove, Jackass penguins either peer watchfully and beady eyed at you from the safety of their burrows, or rush helter skelter, stumbling and sliding on their stomachs, down to the safety of the clear water below.

On a trip over the islands by Beaver floatplane one can frequently see penguin colonies surprisingly far inland, their inhabitants scuttling awkwardly from the sound of the aircraft overhead. From the air, fur seal colonies can also be seen clustered in their hundreds on Volunteer Rocks only a few miles from Stanley, but one is unlikely to see them at close quarters unless you are a roving naturalist like Ian Strange or Maurice Rumboll. After years of depredations by unscrupulous sealers, their numbers are depleted, but since the enactment of a government decree in 1951, the few isolated colonies in the islands are now legally protected and I am sure will remain so in view of the interest aroused over conservation in the islands.

On the tract of land approaching Volunteer Rocks wild cattle, said to date from the time of the gauchos, can be spotted; they are also legally protected.

Sea elephants, with soulful eyes and foetid breath, looking like huge black boulders, flop lazily on shingle beaches. A sea lion is a frequent visitor to the hulk opposite Sulivan House and we would watch him tossing his fish in the air to stun them and listen to him puffing and grunting as he dived and gambolled. We once watched him in fascination as he played tag with two skin divers who got quite a fright. Dolphins also occasionally appeared in the harbour and small schools of them playfully gambolling could he seen at Surf Bay on the opposite side of the harbour.

Throughout the year a variety of scavenging gulls could be seen noisily fighting over mutton scraps and at certain times of the year the shingle along the sea wall would be full of screeching gulls feeding off the pink krill which a combination of wind and tide had brought into the inner harbour and which began to smell a little high after a few days.

It was always interesting to study the activities of pairs of loggerducks, particularly after they had hatched a family and one could watch at close quarters the progress from tiny adorable ducklings to the stage when, grown and ugly, it was chased away by the parents. These fully-fledged loggerducks used to congregate in enormous numbers in Fairy Cove on the other side of the inner harbour and it was fascinating to watch their various disputes over territorial boundaries, though these seldom came to a fight. Usually a display of strength and noisy pretence attacks were sufficient. Like the ancient jousting tournaments of knights in armour, they seldom met. It was always a delight to hear the guttural cry of the female as she raised her head skywards stretching her neck belligerently and the curious piping voice of her mate.

Loggerducks make excellent parents. I once watched a scene from Sulivan House when two tiny ducklings had fallen inside a derelict boat, probably when the tide was high and now that the tide was low were stuck there. The mother duck, in great distress was making a lot of noise. Some workmen nearby rescued them, and as the two ducklings squeaked and swam around in circles looking for mama, who, by then was some distance away, mother loggerduck skimmed the water, almost taking flight in her anxiety to join them, allowing for the fact that she was a flightless steamerduck. The young loggerducks of both sexes which used to congregate in large numbers in Fairy Cove on the opposite side of the harbour to Sulivan House, a well chosen and aptly named spot for the hundreds of young males and females which, prior to mating and establishing their own territorial rights elsewhere fished and made forays together for several months after being driven away by their parents. I was able to watch this ejection take place when 'our' pair of doting parents suddenly turned on their offspring, making venomous darts until they took the hint and finally departed: this lasted for several days as some of the young, more stupid or obstinate than the rest, persisted in attempting to return to the family and would sit a safe distance off distrustfully eyeing the turncoats.

It was amusing to watch a pair of loggerducks put to flight large numbers of young that had the temerity to trespass and the female, always more bellicose than the male, would frequently take on a hundred interlopers single-handed. We would watch them sitting placidly on their favourite rock opposite our house until they became aware of the invading flotilla, whereupon they would set sail in defence of their territory, the irate female in fine voice as she shot through the water or raised her neck and head vertically, uttering her guttural warning, supported by the flute like obligato of her mate. When the pair was close enough to attack the intruders the female loggerduck would streak underwater like a submarine to take the youthful enemy by surprise and put them to flight, routing them with a tremendous flurry of water and flapping of wings. During one bitterly cold spell of weather with blizzard conditions the colony of young loggerducks stole a march and slipped through, unnoticed in the gloom and murk, to forbidden territory for shelter where they sat, huddled on the shingle at the farthest westerly point of our pair's territory. After one furious attack they were allowed on this occasion to stay, so perhaps a truce had been called on account of the unusual weather conditions.

The laying and hatching of eggs always appeared to us a secretive performance, no doubt for reasons of self-preservation, as, contrary to what I was at first led to believe and to what one might expect, loggerduck eggs are said to be good eating. Despite keeping close observation, the female's departure is seldom witnessed and only the unusual sight of the male sitting alone points to her absence. One has to search diligently to find the female sitting on her nest, as she is so well camouflaged in thick tussac grass, or gorse or similar cover that it is rare to find her. Occasionally, the Secretariat female, hers being one of the few nests whose location was known, could be seen waddling clumsily across the main road to join her mate who sat guard on the sea wall while she went fishing before returning to her nest. It was amusing to see Land Rovers stop to allow her to cross the road, so well-known a personality was she and so much interest was there in her annual accouchement.

By the same token logger ducks are said to be inedible on account of their strong fishy flavour, but Sir Francis Drake was evidently glad to make use of them. 'On 24 August we arrived at an island in the streights, where we found great store of foule which could not fly, of the bigness of geese, whereof we killed in lesse than one day 3000 and victualled ourselves thoroughly therewith!'

Six weeks later you might be lucky enough to catch sight of the female proudly leading her newly hatched squad across the road to the water, but the first venture must usually have been made in the small hours as the ducklings were normally first seen bobbing, to the manner born, up and down in the sea like tiny corks, shepherded by proud parents. At the start there would be seven or eight ducklings, but it was never long, despite their parents' vigilance, before these numbers were depleted, gradually, to two or three as the skuas and gulls swooped down for a tasty morsel. One pair near Government House, however, surprisingly kept intact their large predominantly female family, but this was perhaps because they had hatched particularly late in the season.

Male and female characteristics soon appear in the ducklings, revealed by colour of beak and head, and wing markings and, in the female, by the familiar neck and head raising movement. But it is some time before the characteristic cries of the different sexes are distinguishable. Pairs are known as 'the Secretariat loggerducks' and the 'Government House loggerducks'. Stanley residents always show great interest in

11. Loggerducks.

the families produced. The Secretariat pair were perhaps the best known of all as one often had to skirt round them as they sat unmoving on the sea wall, looking as if they owned it, and woe betide anyone who approached too near their brood. I was tempted once to touch one of the fluffy balls, but backed away hastily at the fury of a hissing female.

We were fortunate in being able to witness two logger-duck courtships, one of which took place opposite Sulivan House when the female of the pair came to an untimely end, run over by a Land Rover so it was thought. We watched with curiosity and interest the bereaved male who sat disconsolate on his rock surveying his territory until a teenage female came to court him. After all, he possessed a large territory, one of the largest in Stanley, and was obviously a good catch for any spinster. At first her attentions and intentions were ignored and, even when she persevered, the male continued to angrily drive her away, all part of the elaborate courtship ritual. Eventually, after weeks of forcing her attentions upon him she succeeded, after many rebuffs, as she so well deserved. The previous year we had witnessed a similar courtship of the Government House male loggerduck after the sudden disappearance of his mate. I wonder if the balance of nature is maintained through the large percentage of females born in each family, as the female mortality rate seems to be higher. During our time in Stanley most of the well-known drakes lived, but most of the females died and were replaced. Unfortunately, we did not witness the reverse situation, where the drake dies and his territory is taken over by a younger bird and the widow driven away from the kingdom where she had been joint ruler.

Loggerducks (flightless steamer ducks) are permanent residents, whereas the annual return to Stanley of the young Kelp geese heralds the approach of winter. These birds are indigenous, but migrate to more distant parts of the Falklands for the breeding season. It was a constant delight to admire the magnificence of the Kelp geese on the wing, the snowy splendour of the all-white male contrasting with the jet black of the female dramatically marked with white bars on the wings. Like most females she makes the most noise, honking in flight beside her silent mate. It was also fascinating to watch them delicately peck their way among the green seaweed and a breathtaking spectacle in their graceful flight. It provides a memory which is unforgettable. I was fortunate to witness a flirtation take place on the sea wall one sunny afternoon near the Battle Memorial, a favourite trysting spot for Marines and birds alike. Oblivious of my presence, two males landed nearby and as I froze they were joined by two females, one landing farther along the wall while the second flew straight past me to land only a few feet away beside the male. An exchange of noisy mutterings took place, but no notice was taken of my presence. Then, suddenly, the interlude over, the females flew off in the direction of the nearest jetty, displaying their barred black and white elegance.

The black-browed albatross, or mollymauk to give it its local name, is rarely seen in Stanley, but there are large breeding colonies on some of the other more remote islands. One, which had probably been blown off course by gale force winds, did sit large and clumsily for a few days by the Battle Memorial, obviously too heavy for takeoff from the slope without the assistance of a strong wind. Unfortunately, I missed its departure but saw it later flying low over the harbour. They are very large birds with a great wingspan.

On another occasion, again on the sea wall, a sick penguin appeared for a few days. It stood on the shingle with lustreless eyes and was clearly in very poor condition in marked contrast to this bird's usual jaunty appearance as it scuttles with amazing speed over rocks and sand to dive headlong and swim gracefully in the clear Falkland Islands waters.

Often I used to creep quietly along the rickety jetty leading to the *Jhelum* to spy on a night heron sitting hunched on a rib of the skeleton ship. The bird would take no notice of me except to fluff its feathers and hunch still further on its perch, fixing me with a beady red eye; or, of a still evening, I might come across one delicately stalking an invisible mussel, neck elongated and long pigtail quivering in anticipation, before pouncing on its prey; then, suddenly aware of the intrusion, away it would fly with a long, slow, grey wingbeat giving the bird its characteristic cry, 'quark, quark', the name by which the bird is known locally.

Dainty little grey tufted ducks, which were even more graceful when they took off in formation with a soft whirr of wings, would appear for brief visits near our hulk, in marked contrast to the permanent residents, the great skuas and stinkers, so ugly and ungainly in the water, fighting over mutton scraps which floated down from the butchery. When these ugly scavengers glided at eye level along the sea wall, usually from east to west, it was a sign that the wind was gathering strength for a good blow.

Upland geese, the scourge of the farming community due to their hearty appetite for the same sparse grass needed by the sheep, are so tame that they take little notice of human presence. Heads down, they will continue grazing, oblivious of anything but the precious grass. On one camp trip, we went ashore with the *Darwin*'s captain and crew to Tyssen Island, an uninhabited islet where sheep are left to graze, for an afternoon's shooting of Upland geese to replenish various larders, but it turned out to be more of a slaughter than a sport as the birds took no notice of the visitors nor of the sound of the shots and were consequently mown down from a few yards away. Although very little shooting was done of birds in flight, numbers were wounded and staggered, trailing broken wings, or hopped, trailing broken legs, to collapse and drown in the marshy ground. The hunters abandoned fully as many in this state as they carried away. Later, awaiting the arrival of the scow to take us out to the *Darwin*, the crew sat on the rocks plucking and drawing their trophies, while a beady-eyed, inquisitive Johnny Rook watched them cynically from the roof of the sheep shed. While game usually provides a welcome break from 365, on this occasion we felt disinclined to keep one for our pot.

The name Johnny Rook is said to have arisen from the bird's presence in penguin rookeries, for it has a penchant for penguin eggs. It is also a carrion-eating hawk and, being confined to the Falkland Islands and a few remote islands off Cape Horn, is one of the world's rarest birds of prey. At West Point Island Island, courtesy of the owner Roddy Napier, John was able to see several dozen Johnny Rooks for whom carcasses had been put out on a paddock to ensure their presence in large numbers. They are handsome, golden-black birds, suitably ferocious looking. Other species of carrion-eating birds frequently seen wheeling high in the sky are turkey buzzards and caranchos. Although farmers take every opportunity to shoot these birds of prey, they are scavengers and so perform the same function as the vulture of Africa in keeping the countryside clean of decaying animal matter.

To return to our mutton, or rather our geese, Governor Haskard kept two pairs of Upland geese in the grounds of Government House to mow and manure the lawns. They were, no doubt, an attraction to visitors, as the birds are indigenous to the islands but not normally seen in Stanley. The wings of these two pairs were periodically but insufficiently clipped and consequently they made many attempts to escape.

It became a not uncommon sight for Stanley residents to watch the Governor and his wife, accompanied by reluctant staff, in hot pursuit of the truants, the Governor and his wife, suitably clad in thigh-length fishing waders, striding into the icy waters while their staff shooed and flapped their arms ineffectually from the security of the sea wall; or for the Governor's wife to be seen rowing furiously in a small dinghy in pursuit of an errant male. Eventually, the two females did get away, leaving two disconsolate males behind and vain attempts were made to recruit new mates for them from the camp.

After the Governor's final departure, when John was again Acting Governor, we were delighted to hear that the two remaining prisoners had made their bid for freedom. However, by then Government House staff had been so well trained in dealing with such an event that, like Pavlov's dogs, the chain of reaction was automatically put in motion and the usual announcement reporting their disappearance went over on The Box. We thought no more of the matter until, to our further disappointment, John Bound, the post and telecommunications superintendent, spotted the wanderers by the rifle range and, since their wings were not sufficiently strong to resist pursuit, he was able to grab them and return in triumph to Government House with one under each arm. I fear he did not receive acting gubernatorial congratulations! A further term of imprisonment for the unfortunate birds followed.

A short time after the new Governor's arrival I mentioned to Stan that the Upland geese seemed to have gone AWOL from Government House again. They were no longer in their customary pitch and there followed a certain amount of speculation. Shortly afterwards it came to light in the course of a casual conversation that the geese had found their way into the Government House deepfreeze and subsequently into the pot, a fate they did not deserve and a poor reward for their persistent attempts to regain their freedom. No justice, but Stan confirmed that they would make tough eating!

More than fifty species of bird breed in the Falkland Islands, making them a birdwatcher's paradise and several American professors have taken advantage of the unique opportunity they offer to carry out research. From all accounts, they have found their trips particularly rewarding and some have returned for further visits. Among these are the Pettingills and Professor Wheeler, who are both well known in ornithological circles.

Zoo personnel have been in the habit of making periodic forays to the islands to collect seals, sea elephants, logger ducks and penguins and one of them, Herr Graeber from the Hamburg zoo, was a frequent visitor. However, as interest in conservation increases, the Falkland Islands government has enforced strict measures to limit culling and a local, honorary adviser on conservation has been appointed. In any case, it had always been customary for an inspector, usually John Bound, the superintendent of posts and telecommunications, to accompany collectors to ensure that regulations and catch limitations were observed.

This situation has been due to the efforts of Ian Strange, a name now well known in conservation and wildlife circles and whose books, articles and excellent wildlife paintings have made such an impact, particularly on the American market, as to assist in putting the islands on the map. He has been instrumental in arousing the interest of the World Wildlife Fund and, on the commercial side, of Lindblad Expeditions, whose expensive package tours to the Antarctic on the *Lindblad Explorer* take in several Falkland Island wildlife sanctuaries.

Ian Strange has also recently, in partnership with sympathetic interests, purchased New Island as a nature reserve. This 8000-acre island is ideally suited for the purpose because the majority of Falkland Islands birds, including all five species of penguin, are found there. The black-browed albatross and King shags, both interlopers in the rock hopper penguin colonies, are of additional interest, as are the sea lions and fur seals that breed in the caves below the cliffs. New Island was at one time a scurvy station for whalers and many relics of the old whaling station can still be seen.

Ian Strange was also instrumental in encouraging Len Hill, of penguin millionaire fame, to buy Grand Jason Island and Steeple Jason for £5500 as island reserves. Len Hill, a Gloucestershire ornithologist and self-made tycoon, literally descended on the islands complete with TV teams and equipment, by Argentine naval Albatross amphibian aircraft, to film his newly acquired domain. By this time the islanders were becoming more accustomed to visits by these aircraft, but were disinclined to view with too kindly an eye more than were necessary, coming at a time when the regular twice monthly service from Comodoro Rivadavia had just got under way. In afact, rumours were rife among apprehensive islanders of the possibility of an invasion.

Nor did the penguin millionaire endear himself to the local people by of his attitude. 'So cheap', he chirped, when

12. Argentine Albatross taken from Sulivan House.

interviewed on visitors' corner on 'The Box', referring to his flight to the colony, and then he went on to complain about the export duty on penguins at £12 a head. An offer to fly Len Hill and his TV team, in gratis, on an Argentine naval amphibian aircraft had come through a contact in the Argentine embassy in London; the Foreign and Commonwealth Office had agreed to and accepted it, but without consultation with the Falkland Islands.

So far the Argentine Air Force had collected all the kudos, so the navy was naturally willing to oblige. But, as usual, people not on the spot overlooked the disruption caused in an unsophisticated and undermanned organisation. Resources and manpower were heavily strained on Albatross days, when the capital more or less shut up shop to attend to the arrivals. Beavers were grounded or only flew on a very limited schedule, people involved were diverted from their real jobs, several of them assisted on a voluntary basis, various launches and tugs on fire-fighting duty were diverted for the day, not to mention the unfortunate Danny Borland, the meteorological officer, who had to take on a double shift.

HMS *Endurance* was in Stanley at the time of Len Hill's visit and, not to be outdone by the generosity of the Argentine navy, had to show willing on behalf of the British navy and transport Len Hill and his camera crews to the Jasons. So, all in all, however cheap it was for Len Hill, it was an expensive outing for everyone else concerned. Later, after MV *Forrest* had collected the human and wildlife party from the Jasons, being filmed in the process, two naval Albatross returned to carry them to the mainland, the more junior pilot naturally being delegated the pongy task of freighting the penguins.

The Falkland Islands government was able to take advantage of the arrival of two aircraft to obtain transport via Argentina for some of the schoolchildren bound for schools in that country, thus reducing the pressure of passenger traffic on the regular twice monthly flight schedule, which was already heavily waitlisted. So honours were, on the whole, even. For the first time an air crew encountered a south wind on takeoff from Stanley harbour and we were treated to the sight of a dramatic run from outside the Narrows through that exiguous gap and a takeoff that fed up over the hill just to the east of Stanley over the wireless masts.

Despite the diversity of bird life, by far the greatest attraction for tourists will always be the penguins, and the Falkland Islands are unique in possessing colonies of five species – all except the

Emperor. Rockhoppers are there in their thousands with their bright yellow eyebrow tufts, as are the Jackass penguins so called because they literally bray like donkeys. There are large colonies of the classic Gentoo penguins and Macaroni penguins are present in small numbers, the latter a little larger than Rockhoppers and their eyebrow tufts gold instead of yellow. Then there are the larger, rarer King penguins, which resemble the Antarctic Emperor but are more colourful.

I would like to interpolate here a word of advice about clothing to all potential tourists and visitors to those wind-swept islands. Forget about being elegant. A penetrating wind blows most of the time – anoraks, slacks and sweaters, gum-boots, headscarves and gloves are the daily norm, and windproof garments are essential. Several layers are much better than one thick garment and also have the virtue of being less figure destroying from a woman's point of view. Ankle supporting boots are necessary for walking over rough, uneven tussocky ground. Summer temperatures seldom rise above 12°C. Consequently, there is little variation in temperature throughout the year and the same clothes can be worn, adding or subtracting layers according to what the day brings forth in the way of weather. It is monotonous but practical.

Porpoises and dolphins are still frequently seen cavorting in island waters, but whales, which at one time were a daily sight, are no longer seen, though there have been some recent reports from the settlements of sightings of packs of killer whales. I am reluctant to encroach on what I regard as Ian Strange's preserve, so I will limit my reference to seals to stating that the Falklands have four species – the southern elephant seal, southern sea lion, fur seal and leopard seal.

Various species of animal have been introduced by settlers. Cattle were introduced by the gauchos and horses by the French. Early settlers introduced rabbits and one island is said to be so infested with them that no grass grows. Another island is the haunt of foxes, which John Hamilton introduced from Patagonia, and are a menace to lambs. Pigs were introduced by the French to feed on the tussac grass, but are now extinct. Perhaps Cochon Island had been their home at one time. Sealers introduced goats, but they too are extinct. Guanaco are said to have been introduced from South America in 1862. The John Hamilton estate carried out an experiment to import them from South America in the 1930s, but as there was insufficient feed for them many had to be shot. In 1970, some 60 survivors were counted. The owner of West Point Island kept one as a pet by for a while, but I have recently heard that this guanaco has had to be shot because it had become dangerous and liable to attack visitors.

Hare are common on East Falkland but apparently not on West Falkland. The so-called Falkland Island wolf is extinct. It is thought either to have reached the islands on drift ice from Patagonia or been introduced by Fuegian Indians. The trout in the rivers are not indigenous but are due to the fact that a previous Governor, a keen fisherman, established a small hatchery near Stanley and imported trout to stock the rivers where they give good sport. Mullet and smelt, which abound in Falkland waters, are of excellent quality and are there for the taking – Micky Clark and weather permitting. Over the years, dating from the time of Jules Vernet, several projects for catching, salting and exporting fish to South America have been initiated, but so far nothing has come of them and the rich fishing grounds off the islands are unfortunately left to the Russians. Whale food, or krill, is often found stranded on the islands' beaches in the summer months when large numbers of birds feed like kings.

Fortunately, there are few insects and no bees or wasps to dodge. In fact, the only pest is the bluebottle fly, which, according to the Colonial Annual Report of 1911, under the heading Health, is said to have been introduced to the Falkland Islands on a meat-freezing ship, the SS *Salembria*, in 1878. They are a real danger to health because if they touch meat it immediately becomes flyblown. The slightest hint of warmth in summer brings the flies out in hundreds from their hiding places in cracks and crannies in the stone and wooden work of houses.

One's daily round of activity brings one more in contact with domesticated animals. This is probably because, although constantly busy, there are fewer distractions such as television and daily newspapers, so one has time to absorb and be absorbed by minutiae. With Stan's entourage of tame geese flying down the hill with him from his cottage to our paddock accompanied by his retinue of welcoming hens, semi-wild cats prowling through the paddock to the stables and Mrs Heathman's cow and adopted calf placidly munching turnip tops, Sulivan House often took on the appearance of a farmyard.

One morning we awoke to find that Mrs Heathman's cow had produced a spirily legged calf during the night and mother and daughter both seemed to be doing well. However, on my return from shopping that morning I found everybody plunged in gloom, for a calamity had befallen the newborn calf. It had suddenly gone berserk, as sometimes happens, had jumped the fence, rushed across the road down to the sea wall and plunged into the sea, where it swam frantically towards the hulk and drowned. Fortunately, Rosey, the milkman, had a spare calf, so all ended well.

The idyllic pastoral scene continued with Stan's horses mowing the lawn in summer, an occupation shared at one time by Larry the lamb. Larry was such a pet that he used to follow Stan about like a dog and frequently, even when almost fully grown, used to push his way through the kitchen door of

Sulivan House, quite a feat considering his girth, and stand, looking foolish, his sides heaving, beside his foster father. Larry was also very attached to Mrs Heathman's cow and visibly pined when she was removed from the paddock for a change of scene. Eventually, Larry had to go because he was becoming increasingly dangerous to Mrs Heathman who had become a target and was butted mercilessly when she came down to the paddock in the morning to milk her cow. He was a well-bred Romney ram lamb, so was not relegated to the stockpot.

Later Stan acquired a sweet little brown bull, which was, I think, christened Frederick. He often used to browse on the rich grass behind the house watched over by the black cat until he was old enough to be transferred by schooner to Goose Green. Stan reported that he had walked on board as if he had been doing so every day of his life. Another common sight on the sea wall was the ever increasing flock of semi-wild geese which used to parade solemnly and waken us with their noisy squabbling during the night. They were unusually messy birds but were fairly amiable except when sitting on eggs. At this time the males would stand guard and hiss furiously if you approached. The locals coveted their eggs, but despite this, the flock had increased to a baker's dozen by the time we left. At one time there were large numbers of dogs in Stanley, but after the hydatid disease scare and the enforced quarterly dosing of dogs with Scolaban at the Police Station there was a drastic reduction in their number. As for sheep, they were there in their thousands, all 600,000 of them, all silly.

Chapter 9
Of Cabbages and Kings

There have been many visitors of note to the colony and it is a pity that Stanley has little to show for the many ships and famous faces which have passed that way and stayed awhile by its shores, except for those commemorated in street names and in the names of houses, coves, harbours and schooners. Darwin, Shackleton, Ross and many other Antarctic explorers, scientists, naval officers, as well as the naval brigs, whalers, sealers and great sailing vessels of a bygone age have bequeathed their names.

By proxy, there are Viscount Falkland, first sea lord when the colony was founded and Lord Stanley, secretary of state for the colonies who gave his name to the capital of the islands. Scientists are represented by Hooker's Point, which commemorates the research carried out on the islands' botanical resources. HMS *Sparrow* bequeathed her name to Sparrow Cove as did HMS *Philomel* to Philomel Street, while Hebe Street recalls the brig of that name in which Lieutenant-Governor Moody arrived in the islands, while he in turn gave his name to Moody Brook.

Names of naval ships have been handed down over the years to island's ships and are still represented today in *Clio* and *Philomel*, the latter now a wreck in Fairy Cove. Sulivan

House and Tyssen Island owe their names to naval officers Lieutenant B. J. Sulivan and Lieutenant Thyssen respectively, while Ross Road commemorates the Ross Antarctic expeditions. The Murrel River is named after Murrel Robinson who marked out the town of Stanley. The Tamar Rapids recall the visit of a naval ship and the name Darwin is, of course, represented in several places in the islands. These are a few commemorative names among many.

Apart from the few relics of sailing ships in the small Museum in Stanley, the islands have no other memento of their passing, though many visitors have recorded their impressions, not all of them complimentary. For example, Robert Fitzroy, commander of HMS *Beagle*, who gave his name to one of the farm settlements and to RMS *Darwin*'s predecessor, is recorded in Darwin's diary as considering the colony suitable for a penal settlement – 'a thorough convict colony … fully supplied with necessaries yet without luxuries'. The *Fitzroy* must have had an even worse reputation than RMS *Darwin* because, on being introduced to a retired shipping agent now resident in Buenos Aires, he laughingly remarked that he had witnessed the removal by stretcher of more than one Governor's wife on the ship's arrival at Montevideo from the islands.

Moseley, a naturalist on board the HMS *Challenger* during her famous voyage of 1872, unenthusiastically refers to the stormy, sheep-nibbled Falkland Islands as a 'treeless expanse of moorland and bog, and bare and barren rock' where bitterly cold hailstorms were encountered in summer. Unlike the mutton of today the meat is quoted as 'most excellent' at 3d a pound. Although the quality of the meat has obviously deteriorated, its price, surprisingly, has not risen much over the years. The visitors found that the shepherds in the employ of the Falkland Islands Company were mostly Scots and their cottages were situated every ten miles or so. Although, according to Moseley, the Scots had taken the place of the gauchos who had herded the cattle at the time of Darwin's visit, the gauchos' language and customs had persisted, as they have to some extent to this day.

Comments made by fellow passenger Spry on the wretched and dreary appearance of the settlement of Stanley were even more scathing. Edward Wilson, in his *Diary of the Discovery Expedition to the Antarctic Regions 1901–4*, was struck on his approach to Stanley harbour by the contrasting shades of yellow, green and black highlighted by hail, snowstorms and fitful, intermittent gleams of sunshine. He describes his disappointment at the dismal sight of shanty huts, deserted streets and the lack of welcoming faces. According to Wilson, however, then, as now, there was a plethora of inns still rejoicing in the same names as today, such as the Rose, the Globe and the Ship (now renamed the Upland Goose and where the actress Ellaline Terriss was born). From his reference to an invitation to a 'boring tea-party in Government House', arranged for them to meet the elite of Stanley, he obviously did not rate the hospitality the Governor laid on for them very highly.

The picture drawn is in many ways similar to that of present day Stanley – the deserted streets, old hulks, sleepy atmosphere, the ubiquitous presence of steamer ducks in large numbers, the Falkland Islands Company still enjoys the monopoly they noted, in particular in camp where then, as today, farm hands went to the company store for everything, including postage stamps. Stanley residents had to eat whatever mutton the company thought fit to provide, a complaint of present day Stanley. Refuse from the slaughterhouse littering the environs and nearby shore is noted, as is the complete absence of trees and bushes. Sheep skulls still spoil the shore lines but some attempt at afforestation, however, has now been made in settlements and in the ground immediately behind Government House, while stunted *macrocarpa*, bent low in the direction of the prevailing winds, grow against the shelter of stone dykes. The grass, then as now, was scanty and of poor quality, hard put to meet the demands of one sheep to three acres. Either the sheep today are greedier than their forbears or, more probably, the nutrient value of the herbage has deteriorated, as the number of acres now quoted per sheep is four to five in what is referred to in Wilson's diary as an otherwise 'uninteresting sheep's paradise'.

The south still attracts polar research scientists and intrepid yachtsmen lured by the thrill and vast loneliness of watery wastes and the struggle with the elements; the Falkland Islands now, as always, proves a useful staging post. Among recent visitors was a lone yachtsman known in the colony as Rusty who arrived on his yacht *Flydd* to make repairs, gather supplies and rest before venturing round the Horn. During his short stay he became a popular figure and it was with great sadness that the inhabitants of Stanley came to realise that this was to be his last journey on seeing his yacht, on its way down the inner harbour to the Narrows, suddenly veer unexpectedly onto the rocks to port of the harbour exit as he was restarting his round the world voyage. Rusty had suffered a heart attack and had died, as all true sailors like to go, at the helm. After his burial in Stanley cemetery on a fine yachtsman's day of sun and fair wind, a recording he had made before he sailed provided a moving tribute to his passing.

During his two lengthy stays in Stanley, the islanders adopted the Italian sailor Giovanni Ajmone-Cat as one of their own. He arrived a tall, bearded, swarthy, deceptively piratical figure in nautical rig and sea boots in a lateen rigged felucca type yacht called *San Giuseppe Due*. The inhabitants received him initially with reservation, as it was known he had spent some time in Argentine ports before arriving in Stanley, to stay several months strengthening his sails and deckhouse and generally preparing the *San Giuseppe Due* for the ordeal ahead in the Antarctic. It was to be the first time a ship of this rig had sailed so far south. His book on his epic journey south is soon to be published and if his description of the raging seas near Cape Horn, the gigantic troughs, the solemn grandeur of cathedral vaults of ice and snow are anything to go by, his book should be a best seller.

He was persuaded to postpone his planned departure south until the British Antarctic Survey ships were in the area and everyone became alarmed at one stage when radio contact with the *San Giuseppe Due* was lost. She was eventually contacted at Deception Island where the ship was sheltering after the buffeting she received on the southern voyage. During this time the two young members of the crew had become disenchanted with their task and the Chilean ice-breaker, *Pablo Pardo*, lifted them out from Deception while Ajmone-Cat remained alone on his boat awaiting the arrival of crew replacements from Italy. Through his contacts there he was able to conjure up replacements consisting of two senior Italian naval ratings and a friend, an experienced pilot with Alitalia, was given leave to come and assist with the navigation; the armed services of Argentina brought them down to the Antarctic. On his return to Stanley, Ajmone-Cat remained for a considerable time patching up his vessel before once again sailing, this time for Europe, taking with him a Falkland Islander as crew member, I understand that the lure of the Antarctic was such that he has planned another southern expedition and will, as I write, be on his way to the Falkland Islands again.

During our second season, the Joint Services Expedition under Commander Burley of the Royal Navy, nicknamed Micro-Shack, arrived in Stanley on HMS *Endurance*. He spent a few days in Stanley before leaving for Elephant Island in the Antarctic, there to re-enact step by step, Shackleton's journey to safety. Their brief visit to Stanley was an ideal opportunity for the team to try out its equipment, but, as luck would have it, they hit a warm patch of weather and found a crosscountry tramp in Antarctic gear rather trying. We watched them stepping out past Sulivan House one Sunday morning laden with gear and already pink with exertion.

The arrival of so much shipping during the season brought birds of a different feather to the colony, as well as our first visitors from Argentina, which many islanders interpreted as the thin end of the wedge. General Lathbury, a former Governor of Gibraltar, arrived on HMS *Endurance* to spend the season aboard, staying periodically in Government House between sailings. He was a popular figure on board and endeared himself to the crew by insisting on being treated informally and, whenever accommodation on board was limited, to turning in with the crew. He had a keen interest in birds and, during his short visits to Stanley, could frequently be seen walking along the sea wall with his binoculars at the ready.

Another arrival by BAS ship was Admiral Irvine, the oceanographer, a tiny, bird-like, lively man of impish appearance. He was on a trip south on the RRS *John Biscoe* with his old friend and colleague on the Antarctic committee of the National Environmental Research Committee, Sir Vivian Fuchs, who is practically an annual visitor to the Falkland Islands and well known by everyone there. Despite his charisma and aura of intrepid Antarctic explorer, Bunny Fuchs, as he is popularly known, is a very human, kindly, likeable person, never happier than when he is on his way south to his old stamping grounds.

Ex-Governor Arthur of the Falkland Islands also made a brief visit to his former fief on the *Lindblad Explorer*. Governors are not permitted to visit the scene of former Governorships until at least five years had passed, but Governor Arthur had been away for a great deal longer than this. A special party was arranged for him at Government House to enable him to renew his old island acquaintanceships.

Much later, well after the end of the season, the Right Honourable Stanley came on the MV *AES* with a strange retinue of companions. Already a sick man, he had arrived with a mission to hand over to Government House a volume which had belonged to his ancestor who had given his name to the colony's capital.

Last but not least of a selected list of VIPs was Sir Michael Hadow, our ambassador to Argentina and, to avoid undue publicity in Argentina, he came on the *Lindblad Explorer*. At that time the name 'Argentina' still evoked unpleasant emotions among islanders and many of the inhabitants viewed Sir Michael's first visit to the colony with suspicion. It had to be explained rather forcibly that he was British. The ambassador was unlucky with the weather on his visits; on this occasion he visited the camp, hoping at the same time to fit in some fishing and shooting, but had the misfortune to be stormbound at the settlement of Port Howard for days on end in such adverse weather conditions that the Beavers were unable to fly.

On his second visit, when he travelled to the islands by the Argentine cruise ship *Argentina*, the call at Stanley was kept secret from the other passengers until the last minute, probably to avoid exciting any undue patriotic fervour on the part of the Argentinians, Sir Michael went down with a virulent islands flu bug. Another spell of bad weather followed, which put a stop to flying for several days and this again put paid to his intended fishing expedition. However, on both occasions, he was able to meet and get to know islanders and to sound out local opinion at first hand on the 'problem' initially and subsequently the Argentine–Islands rapprochement, and to become sufficiently well known locally for people to feel that they had in him a useful and friendly ally in Buenos Aires. This was the first time that any firm link with Argentina had been seen to be established.

The arrival on RMS *Darwin* of Señor Moreno and his wife, however, once again cast a shadow, for Señor Moreno, a well-known Argentine journalist, writer and lecturer was noted for his hard-line attitude on the problem. Many years earlier, he had visited the Falklands and had written a slim book on the subject called *Nuestras Malvinas*. I understand he upset his fellow passengers on the *Darwin* by ostentatiously displaying his book, and its title, while walking on deck. His mild, bespectacled appearance belied the attitude disclosed in his writings and his wife seemed the more vociferous of the two about their opinions. The normal facilities had been requested on behalf of the Morenos, particularly introductions to leading personalities, and to us therefore fell this awkward task. It proved to be as difficult as we anticipated because local people, still firmly anti-Argentine, were reluctant to talk to, or be seen to be talking to, these visitors who epitomised the hated foreign attitude. The Governor and his wife had to tread warily and so it fell to the Colonial Secretary and his wife, to me in particular as I spoke Spanish, to undertake the invidious task of entertaining them in a hostile environment.

The Morenos used RMS *Darwin* as a floating hotel so there was no accommodation problem. One morning I invited them to Sulivan House for coffee, brandy and a private chat. This had the intended effect of disarming them to some extent, as well as enabling me to confine the conversation to strictly non-political subjects. Señor Moreno took colour photographs of his wife and me against the background of gay flowers in our sunny conservatory. One of these photographs subsequently appeared as an illustration in an article he wrote about his visit to the islands in a popular Argentine magazine, *La Nación*. Due to the usual difficulties over mail between the colony and Argentina, however, I did not know about it at the time and did not receive a copy until many months later, long after my return from Buenos Aires, where I had been ostensibly incognito and parrying natural curiosity about the reasons for my visit

I met Señor Moreno one afternoon in Stanley and took him into the gymnasium where a display of fruit and vegetables for the flower show was being prepared and he was able to talk for a few minutes to A. G. Barton, of *Keep the Falklands British* fame, and to exchange a few polite niceties. Señor Moreno was delighted with the stand displaying vegetables from the Government House garden and took several photographs, much to the Governor's annoyance, who later claimed that his turnips had been misrepresented.

Later during the Morenos' visit we gave a cocktail party at Sulivan House, being neutral ground, for the visitors to meet members of the Legislative and Executive Councils and other leading islands personalities, including the Governor and the ambassador. The party got off to a sticky start until my mint juleps took effect, after which things went more smoothly, though with most of the islanders being very cagey and avoiding saying more than a few words while Señora Moreno monopolised the attention of Sir Michael. The first step had now been taken in welcoming Argentinians, but one could hardly claim to have broken the ice as the visit was not a success. A certain amount of hostility was engendered by it and by Señor Moreno's subsequent article.

It was at about this time that Reynaldo Reid, the sole Argentinian national living in the colony, decided to visit Buenos Aires to register his recently born son as an Argentine citizen, thus making the first reverse visit from the islands. Reid and his wife, leaving the baby boy in Stanley, went to Montevideo by RMS *Darwin* and from there across to Buenos Aires where they were given a rapturous welcome by the Argentine press. It was, from the Argentine point of view, a good publicity scoop, but too much was made of the incident, which culminated in an interview with the President. The whole affair did not go down at all well in the islands.

Although a start had been made in reciprocal visits the unfortunate and partly fortuitous selection of visitors was not auspicious for the future. It often seemed to those on both sides who were working so hard to improve relations that it was a case of one step forward and two steps back. As it was, the groping gestures which had taken place merely created eddies and undercurrents of rumour and suspicion.

Shortly after this visit Sir Michael Hadow departed for Punta Arenas in southern Chile on the RRS *John Biscoe* along with the Haskards who were to tranship in the Chilean port to HMS *Endurance* for their last Antarctic visit as High Commissioner. An interesting aside is that protocol requires the Admiralty to give permission for a female to travel on a naval ship. An immutable naval custom also demands that any female passenger be locked in her cabin at night.

We saw them off from the Public jetty in the howling gale usually associated with such departures, after reassuring the master, John Cole, who was in a tizzy over the protocol regarding precedence in seating arrangements at his table as he had both a Governor and an Ambassador on board. On this occasion the Union Jack instead of the silly Falkland Islands sheep waved from Sulivan House flagstaff, as with the Governor still in his territory, John became Deputy Governor at the princely additional sum of £1 a day.

During the later rather lengthy interregnum, while John was Acting Govenor and High Commissioner, between the departure of the old Governor and the arrival of the new one, our next Argentine visitors were allowed into the colony. The policy of opening up the islands to a selected few Argentines was now under way and it was hoped that these two visitors from the Argentine media would have a sensible approach and, in due course, represent the islands sympathetically in their magazine.

We were about to meet two practising journalists, or rather, one journalist and his accompanying photographer. Their article and photographs subsequently appeared in the popular magazine *Gente*, the equivalent of a lurid *Picture Post*, which was a disappointment because we had expected them to appear in one of the expensive Argentine glossies, *Atlantida*, which would have called for a different approach for a more sophisticated readership. As it was, the photographs were particularly cruel and the article, though apt, had a mordant bite. I assessed the article and its possible impact. The authors had, with rare insight into island character, picked out the salient features of local personalities from the Governor downwards and cleverly interpreted their characters, but the result, though true up to a point, gave a distorted picture and a false impression to outsiders. The intention had been good, but the application poor and the islanders were displeased with the impression given by the journalists.

The Argentine government at last hit the right note with its next choice of visitor whose arrival almost coincided with that of the new Governor. Colonel Huarte and his wife along with an elderly artist arrived on RMS *Darwin* for a lengthy visit, which included several camp trips. They had clearly been selected in an effort to counteract the unfortunate impression created by the Morenos and the two journalists. The choice could not have been bettered. They were immediately popular and made a definite impact on everybody they met. The Huartes were a pleasant, unassuming, middle-aged couple; a retired army colonel, Señor Huarte was human and readily likeable and he and his wife, a handsome woman, beautiftilly groomed in the Buenos Aires manner, were both very *simpático*.

The artist, true to his profession, set up his easel and could be seen, even in bitterly cold weather, sketching Stanley views. He soon attracted interested spectators from passers-by, which was probably the object of the exercise because, through him, contact was made with many islanders and he and the Huartes were invited into Falkland Islands homes both in Stanley and in the camp. This enabled them to meet and talk to a cross section of the community. They made friends during their stay and now take a keen interest in the welfare of Falkland Islands schoolchildren attending British schools in Buenos Aires. Their stay also coincided with the mercy flight to Stanley by an Argentine air force Albatross amphibian aircraft, so on this occasion Argentine visitors were able to leave with a feeling that lost ground had been retrieved. For the first time a visit had ended successfully, which must have given much personal satisfaction to Colonel and Señora Huarte, whose manner had been primarily responsible for its success. A turning point had been reached. It was now possible to feel that with careful selection of visitors of the right calibre, so long as their number did not suddenly escalate, even the hardliners among the islanders would come to accept that people from the mainland did not all have tails and cloven hooves.

Once plans were afoot to operate a temporary air service from Argentina, more Argentine faces were seen in the colony. Among them was a nurse, Cristina Fooks, from the British hospital in Buenos Aires who came to help out during a period of staff shortages in the government hospital in Stanley. She encountered some local bias and was lonely at first until Lynda Chapman, the personal assistant at Government House and

Audrey Gann, a member of John's staff who was in the colony for a year under British Technical Assistance, took her under their wing. This kindness Cristina was later able to reciprocate in full during the British girls' stay in Argentina at the end of their tours of duty in the colony.

A gradual change in attitudes took place to the extent that, when an Argentine cruise ship called at Stanley for the first time with the British ambassador on board, passengers were welcomed ashore and the head of the Malvinas and Antarctic department of the Argentine foreign ministry, Señor Izaguirrez, came ashore to attend a formal dinner party at Government House. What had for so long been a slow movement was at last gathering momentum.

Chapter 10

Great Britain Will Enter Harbour

While the Governor and Lady Haskard were down south on HMS *Endurance* enjoying the splendours of the peninsula's ice floes and glaciers, we had our own spot of excitement in Stanley with the absorbing first stages of the *Great Britain* affair. On 25 April 1970 the West German tug *Varius II*, towing its massive pontoon *Mulus III*, arrived in Stanley harbour with Lord Strathcona on board. A leading member of the *Great Britain* project committee, he was to oversee the venture. His brother-in-law Jamie Chewton, who was covering the story for *The Times*, accompanied him.

After an earlier visit by three tough, outspoken salvage experts from Hull, who were dubious about a salvage operation, particularly one involving towing the *Great Britain* on her own hull, the salvage experts Risdon Beasley had suggested the Hamburg company of Ulrich Harms to undertake the task of towing Isambard Kingdom Brunel's ship on a pontoon, a technique they had developed to a high stage of efficiency. As luck would have it, one of their tugs, with a pontoon, was already on its way to West Africa and, after completion of its assignment on the coast, was instructed to sail on to the islands by way of Montevideo. This was bad luck on the crew who were hardly equipped, after a visit to West Africa, for Falkland Islands weather. Euan Strathcona and Jamie Chewton joined the ship in Montevideo as did the five-man salvage team from Risdon Beasley under Leslie O'Neil, no stranger to the islands and now able to renew acquaintanceships made during his stay there in the last war as a member of the crew of HMS *Exeter*. Last but not least, though no doubt the smallest, came Horst Kaulen, the brilliant young pontoon salvage expert from Germany.

Brunel's brainchild of 1843, the first iron built, screw driven, oceangoing ship, had sadly ended her days in Stanley harbour, joining the numerous picturesque wrecks and hulks gathered there after fighting their losing battles with the sea and weather round Cape Horn. For a while she had been used as a wool store, but since 1936 had been beached in Sparrow Cove, a few miles out of Stanley harbour. She had spent the latter part of her career under sail and three huge masts, the largest sailing ship masts ever built, were to pose formidable problems for the salvage experts. The project committee donated one of these masts to Stanley as a memorial to the *Great Britain*'s sojourn in Falkland waters. As involuntary custodians for so many years, Falkland Islanders visiting Britain are welcome on board the ship to see the latest renovations. Throughout the salvage operation, the Falkland Islands detachment of Marines under the command of Captain Malcolm Macleod, who were nearing the end of their year's tour of duty, lived up to their reputation by assisting in a hundred and one different ways as did many islanders who were anxious to help in any way possible with 'their ship'.

After a number of disheartening setbacks which might have put off a less strong-willed and dedicated team, on a cold, grey wet and windy day the *Great Britain* was, to most people's relief, safely floated onto *Mulus III* and towed in triumph into Stanley harbour, to be greeted by ringing bells, blowing car horns and All-Stanley with their cameras at the ready. To watch the negotiation of the Narrows by this unusual and bulky tow was to witness a piece of seagoing history as the unique and awe-inspiring sight of Brunel's proud creation towering atop the leviathan pontoon loomed up through the misty rain.

Later that day the weather deteriorated and by evening the wind had reached gale force, with driving squalls of hail, sleet and snow. Several anxious hours were spent as the tug rode out the storm, which continued throughout the night; the pontoon, with *Great Britain* atop, at times swinging dangerously on her anchor, drifted hazardously near the rocks on the other side of the harbour. Meanwhile, Lord Strathcona and his brother-in-law were somewhat apprehensively toasting the success of the venture in Chilean champagne at Sulivan House to a Wagnerian accompaniment of howling wind, hailstones battering against the windows as we piled more peat onto the fire. The *Great Britain*, no ship to do things by halves, was living up to her reputation as 'the biggest and the best' by celebrating her rebirth in the storm of the year. To everyone's relief, it was still there the next morning as well as an exhausted tug captain who had not slept for 36 hours. That evening the tug and pontoon came alongside the east jetty.

Over the next ten days, while welding and other work was being carried out to ensure the *Great Britain*'s safety for the journey home, the islanders were hoping to collect bucketfuls of the *Great Britain*'s mussels, which were considered a real delicacy. Unfortunately, however, they were found to have been contaminated by oil. They were inedible and the atmosphere became rather high as they dried out in the wind.

By this time the Governor and Lady Haskard had returned to Stanley from the Antarctic on HMS *Endurance* and on 23 April Sir Cosmo Haskard, in a formal ceremony, held in the shadow of the hull of the *Great Britain*, with a large audience of Stanley inhabitants, some of them with British flags last used to emphasise a point during Lord Chalfont's visit, and schoolchildren, handed over to Lord Strathcona the documents transferring the crown wreck to the *Great Britain* project committee.

Several other gifts were made, including a barometer which had belonged to the ship's captain, donated by Miss Madge Biggs, a bath from the ship that had lain behind the Secretariat until John decided to return it to its original nautical home and several other items to form the nucleus of objects for the ship's museum, or for those cabins and other parts of the ship that would eventually, for the benefit of the public, be restored to their original magnificence. A lighter touch was introduccd with the handing over, after the official ceremony, of a mysterious brown paper parcel. This contained the spare sets of underwear that Lord Strathcona and Viscount Chewton, who had been spending a few days at Government House as guests of the Governor, had been frantically trying to track down prior to their imminent departure.

On the morning of 24 April, as if to make up for the recent inclement weather, the sun shone brightly. It was a moving and impressive sight to watch from the hill high above Stanley the stately progress of the tug and the towering bulk of the *Great Britain* through the Narrows to the wider waters of Port William and the open sea beyond, the sea ashimmer with light, the flash of the scarlet Beaver in the blue sky as it dipped in salute, and the hovercraft spreading its skirt low in the water in a deep curtsy in homage at her passage, buzzed an accompaniment as the *Great Britain* made her triumphant exit from those waters where it had for so long been a forlorn prisoner.

This epic journey of the *Great Britain* also marked the end of the season. The traditional camp trip undertaken by the

13. Alongside a camp settlement.

Governor and his wife on HMS *Endurance* was over and had been dogged by bad weather; on one occasion, I understand, the navy was forced to steam up and down Berkeley Sound throughout the night, unable to drop anchor because of gale force winds. At each settlement, the ship anchored some distance off, there being few deep water harbours, and visits to and from shore were made by launch. At one settlement a storm blew up while the Governor and Lady Haskard, General Lathbury and party were ashore. Conditions were such that it was out of the question for them to return to the ship until the next day and the party visiting the ship was similarly storm-bound, with an ensuing confusion of sheets, blankets and bunks at both ends.

I have heard that one Governor, when visiting the camp, was in the habit of appearing in full gubernatorial dress, but that the campers were not particularly impressed. On the whole, camp trips of this kind tended to be relaxed and fairly informal, showing the flag to the people in the settlements and giving them the opportunity to entertain and be entertained by the Governor and the Navy. It also provided relaxation for the crew in the form of shooting, riding and fishing at the end of an arduous Antarctic season.

A round of farewell cocktail and dinner parties celebrated in a spirit of euphoria before the ships sailed north for home followed the annual camp trip. HMS *Endurance* left with the five-man agricultural team on board, to be helicoptered ashore at Rio Gallegos in Argentina to begin a short but marathon tour of Argentinian and Chilean *estancias* and *frigoríficos* before returning to Britain to write their report.

The departure of the outgoing detachment of Marines also took place on the Public jetty amid tearful scenes, but the new detachment was already settling in and getting the lie of the land. At the end of each season there would be a number of Falkland brides preparing to leave the colony, like the *Great Britain*, for better or for worse.

Chapter 11
South American Tango

At the end of June 1970 the Colonial Secretary and his wife had a welcome break. The first round of talks with Argentina dealing with the problem was to be held at the Foreign and Commonwealth Office with Falkland Islands representation which was one of its most important features as the achievement in securing this representation in the climate of opinion prevailing in the colony at the time, is not to be underestimated. The Colonial Secretary was to head the Falkland Islands delegation and Dick Goss, as senior elected member of the colony's legislature was selected to represent the islands. Robin Pitaluga, farm manager and joint owner of Salvador station on East Falkland and also a member of the Executive and Legislative Councils, who was already on holiday in Britain with his family, would join them as the third member.

I was to go as far as Buenos Aires, to spend a week incognito before returning to Montevideo for five weeks to await John's return and the next southward sailing of RMS *Darwin*. Among those leaving the colony for good were Padre Millam and his family, the Stainer family and the Governor's personal assistant Sarah Swanick. Others, like Ray Clements of the British Antarctic Survey, were going on leave.

On any outgoing *Darwin* a large crowd would congregate and board the ship to celebrate departures, and this was expected to be quite a gay sendoff. However, as we approached the jetty we noticed the Falkland Islands Company's flag at half mast and a distinct air of gloom as we set foot on the gangway; a senior member of the crew had died on board that morning. With memories of a wreath I began to think that we were fated. It was a distinctly odd feeling watching the crowd on the quayside and Stanley recede into the distance as we sailed through the Narrows, I had not expected such a reprieve in our three-year tour and it was a relief to escape some of the winter. The day was grey and cheerless and the wind had an icy bite. Sadie Clements and I, both poor sailors, had decided to experiment with strips of Elastoplast behind the ears, recommended as a sure cure for seasickness. Sadie persevered with her Elastoplast strips, but once into the open sea the *Darwin* started to buck and, feeling myself turning green, I retired rapidly to my bunk where the Elastoplast soon came off. It was, as usual, a rough trip and I spent a good part of it flat on my back, wedged into the bunk while, with aching muscles, I braced myself against the violent movements of the ship. Twenty-four hours out of Montevideo came resurrection, as the climate grew milder and we sailed up the River Plate in brilliant sunshine.

John and I, with Dick Goss, were to leave Montevideo the same evening for Buenos Aires on the night ferry which we had deliberately chosen as our mode of transport. This fitted in with our arrival in Montevideo as we were in the same dock area and thus did not entail having to go through Customs. It was also as well to evaluate every system of transport between Montevideo and Buenos Aires for future reference. My presence as interpreter was necessary in case we ran into difficulties, despite the careful diplomatic arrangements that had been made.

We were able to transfer to the *Ciudad de Buenos Aires*, a large, modern, bright-blue ferry, shortly after completing immigration formalities on board HMS *Darwin*. Alberto Ward of McLean & Stapledon had come aboard *Darwin* to meet us on arrival and to see us safely over to the *Buenos Aires*. The Argentine government had assured us that the immigration formalities would present no difficulty; in fact, the immigration officials seemed disinterested in us or our passports and after the most casual of scrutinies, we went aboard feeling rather like spies at large.

Falkland Islands passports are unacceptable in Argentina because, in Argentine eyes, to accept them would amount to recognition of the separateness of the islands and abandonment of Argentina's claim to sovereignty. There was no reason why John and I should be considered anything other than British tourists visiting Argentina, as neither of our British passports bore a stamp indicating that we had landed in the Falkland Islands. Such a stamp is normally only entered at the request of the individual (a popular tourist gimmick for passport stamp collectors) but, in the same way as it is a disadvantage for someone visiting an Arab country in the Middle East to have a passport bearing an Israeli stamp, it is likely to prove embarassing in certain circumstances.

We had also gone to great trouble to ensure that our international health certificates were blameless in Argentine eyes. When my smallpox vaccination certificate expired, the renewal stamp was so organised so as to omit reference to the Falkland Islands, which was no doubt a judicious illegality. I later went through a similar procedure to renew my international yellow fever certificate, which was done aboard HMS *Endurance* to provide anonymity. It was advisable, when travelling through Argentina, to avoid carrying documentation bearing Falkland Islands official stamps, as one never knew when some hot-headed, hardlining, minor official might throw a fit of temperament. We were taking no chances. Later, when John had his smallpox certificate renewed in Buenos Aires while we were travelling through South America on our way back to Europe at the end of our Falklands assignment, we were impressed with the speed and efficiency with which the Argentine health service operated, so very different from our normal experience of South American bureaucracy, with which we were to have had ample dealings before we saw the continent for the last time.

Dick had a British passport because he had been taken to the islands as a child, but 'Stanley, Falkland Islands' was entered as his place of residence. It was precisely to gloss over this that concerted arrangements with the Argentine authorities had been made. Because a female colleague distracted the immigration official at the kiosk on board the *Ciudad do Buenos Aires* just at the moment our passports were presented to him, with Dick's carefully sandwiched between mine and John's, he gave them only the most cursory glance. Assuming that all was well and not wishing to call undue attention to ourselves on this, our first contact with Argentine soil, we shrugged our shoulders South American style and made our way to our roomy and well-appointed cabins.

To avoid the football crowds returning to Buenos Aires from Montevideo, we decided to have an early meal using Argentine pesos borrowed from Alberto Ward, followed by a drink in the crowded bar, a walk round the spacious deck, before retiring to our cabins soon after 9.00 p.m. We went to bed to the accompaniment of a continuous stream of announcements over the public address system and were almost asleep when we heard a call for Señor and Señora Jones y Mayor Goss to report immediately to the immigration bureau. An agitated, half undressed Dick Goss came knocking at our cabin door, but we sent him back to bed with soothing advice to ignore the summons, assuring him that I would deal with the matter in the morning. My presence was after all turning out to be necessary. After a few attempts to winkle us out, the message was no longer repeated until, first thing in the morning, came the same urgent summons.

I sallied forth, fighting my way through the crowd, which was already queueing up in preparation for the dash ashore, to find a friendly but obviously worried official who wanted our three passports returned to him. I persuaded him to come to our cabin rather than leave me to fight my way through the mêlée twice more. It transpired that Dick's passport had been stamped with an entry visa, which presented quite a problem to the official, who was faced with a British passport which nevertheless contained a domicile in the Falkland Islands and now bore an Argentine stamp, which acknowledged that there was a place named the Falkland Islands and not Las Malvinas. However, something else was obviously bothering him because he continued to examine the three passports and their photographs with some perplexity and to subject me to close scrutiny. We realised, from his questions, that Dick's passport carried his wife's photograph and, since Dot Goss was a Falkland Islander, the official was making quite sure that I was me and not her. The illogicality of the exercise was beyond me as I had very obviously slept in the Col. Sec.'s cabin; but such are the tortuous ways of officialdom! At last he appeared satisfied and went off bearing Dick's passport, which was later returned with a cancellation stamp covering the earlier entry visa but, because the original was in indelible ink, not obliterating it. Honour was satisfied and Dick Goss now has a unique memento of his first visit to Argentina.

On arrival in Buenos Aires, embassy officials, including the counsellor Murray Hunter, met us bearing the news that the

Conservatives had won the election in Britain, which Dick found a bit of a damper at eight o'clock in the morning of his first day in Argentina, and that General Levingston had replaced General Ongania as president of Argentina, as one periodical described it as 'yet one more general in and out the revolving doors of the Casa Rosada'. We were whisked off for a welcome breakfast with Sir Michael Hadow at the Casa de Madeira in the heart of Buenos Aires, and were not surprised to see that the army was out in force.

While John and Dick had briefing sessions in the embassy, I was taken to the British Council to see what they had in store for me – a full programme of visiting Anglo-Argentine schools, the British hospital and an Argentine teacher training college. I returned to the Residency to an official lunch where everyone, Argentine and British embassy officials and Argentine and British businessmen alike, were interested in and avid for information about the islands. Later that afternoon John and Dick left from Ezeiza airport, 20 miles from the capital, for London. There were no hitches this time with immigration formalities because the arrangements were in the competent hands of Tom Evans, an Anglo-Argentine of Welsh ancestry and the embassy genie of travel arrangements.

A hectic week of visits followed for me and included the Buenos Aires social whirl, which appeared to take place every night of the week. My year in the islands had taken more out of me than I had expected and I flagged rapidly. Realising this, Mrs Findlay, the British Council liaison officer and wife of a leading member of the British business community, who accompanied me on my visits, literally carried me through the rest of the week.

One amusing cloak and dagger experience occurred when I wanted to change some travellers' cheques to pay for my return ferry journey to Montevideo. 'No bother', said the embassy staff nonchalantly, but changed its tune when I informed them, tongue in cheek, that 'they would have to think it out again' because these travellers cheques were issued by the banking branch of the Falkland Islands Company and bore the company's name stamp. This put them on the spot as they had to 'arrange', at top level, 'a small transaction'. But it was as well that they should be aware of all the difficulties which could arise for visitors from the islands.

One agreeable surprise meeting was with the newly arrived third secretary in the embassy, Elizabeth Ogilvie. We had been in the same year at Edinburgh University and, though we had only known each other there by sight, recognition signals went out and contact was soon established. Elizabeth was later to make a useful visit to the colony with which, on account of her childhood background in the Hebrides, she felt a close affinity.

The week over, I thankfully flopped into my bunk on the small night ferry back to Montevideo and so to my good friends Margit and Henri Bondonneau in Carrasco where, for the next five weeks. I was looked after, cossetted and fussed over while I relaxed in the gracious atmosphere of their lovely home and soaked up the sun. I enjoyed re-establishing contact with Montevideo, with which I had felt a rapport from the start. I was able to do some useful shopping, have clothes cleaned, shoes mended and a hairdo – in brief, all the things one lacked in the islands. High among these was the pleasure of eating out in good restaurants, walking along the beach at Carrasco, and taking trips into town by car with Margit or sometimes on my own in one of Montevideo's rickety old buses.

Uruguay was in a state of emergency at the time because of the operations of the Tupamaros, so passports or identity cards had to be carried and soldiers bristling with sub-machine-guns would often stop cars at roadblocks. Whenever I went into town by bus I would take the precaution of leaving all my jewellery behind and carrying very little money, as the Tupamaros had recently held up a bus and taken handbags and personal items of value from the passengers.

As a follow-up to the visits I had made in Buenos Aires, I visited the British hospital in Montevideo, to which serious cases from the islands were sent, and the British school, which was attended by a number of Falkland Islands children, as well as Falkland House where the children boarded, forming a small Falkland Islands' expatriate community. I was astonished to see how white they were and was told that they seldom went out until the sun had lost its heat.

On their return from London, John and Dick Goss were delayed in Buenos Aires for further meetings at the embassy. Then, while I chafed at the unexpected delay a few miles away across the River Plate, they were coerced into attending the Palermo show and the Buenos Aires social round. Eventually, an embassy car arrived to take me to Carrasco airport. Instead of the few days we had expected to be in the Colombia Palace Hotel awaiting the *Darwin*'s departure, our stay was reduced to a single night. This was a relief for John because, though the Falkland Islands government covered his expenses, they did not cover mine. The next afternoon, after stocking up with cheese and garlic sausage for our arrival in Stanley, we climbed aboard *Darwin*, this time as old hands.

It was the beginning of August and the ship was fairly full of new arrivals, islands students from Britain on their biannual holiday and a few islanders, who were soon to he seen relaxing in their carpet slippers, a Falkland Islands custom. It was now midwinter; the passage was rough and, after the first 36 hours, I was not seen again for the rest of the journey. In fact, I disgraced myself by not getting out of my bunk until after we had passed through the Narrows, a few minutes before tying up alongside the east jetty.

Stan was there to greet us and while John went with the new personal assistant to Government House to give his impressions of the talks, I retired to Sulivan House to organise the hot water bottles. To my surprise, our return was marked by a sense of homecoming. The welcome break had set me up for the rest of our tour and I returned physically and mentally alert, looking forward to the politically more interesting prospect which the first round of talks had opened up.

Chapter 12
The Party is Over

There followed lengthy sessions in the Council Chamber in Government House with Executive and Legislative Councils, or 'parliament' as Stan called it.

Executive Council consists of the Governor as chairman with a mixture of *ex officio*, elected and appointed members. It is the colony's cabinet. In 1969 it consisted of:

Sir Cosmo Haskard	Chairman	
J. A. Jones	Colonial Secretary	senior member
L. C. Cleadell	Colonial Treasurer	member
Major R. V. Goss	elected member	
R. M. Pitaluga	elected member	
A. G. Barton	appointed member	
S. Miller	appointed member	

The elected members of the Executive Council are elected to it by the elected members of the Legislative Council. The law stipulates that the Colonial Secretary and Colonial Treasurer serve as *ex officio* members, that two members are elected in the manner indicated and that the Governor appoints two members. The constitution does not specify from where the two appointed members must come. Some people believed it was conventional to have one from East Falkland and one from West Falkland, but this is not so, though it has sometimes happened that way fortuitously.

Leaving aside the *ex officio* members of the 1969 Executive Council, in the Legislative Council Goss (an elected member) represented Stanley, Pitaluga East Falkland, S. Miller West Falkland and Barton (though not a member of the Legislative Council) represented Stanley. Soon after being elected to the Legislative Council for West Falkland, S. Miller retired from his job as manager of a West Falkland farm and came to live in Stanley. This perhaps gave the impression that Stanley had three 'representatives' on the Executive Council – Goss, Miller and Barton – though Miller was always at pains to make it clear that he was a Wester. In any case, the word 'representation' is a misnomer so far as the Executive Council is concerned. The task of members of the Executive Council is to give the best advice they can to the Governor; the word 'representative' properly belongs to membership of the Legislative Council.

Early in 1969, mainly because of the Governor's need for rapid access to both his Executive and Legislative Councils due to political difficulties with Argentina, the experiment was tried of the two councils sitting together. When sitting in its executive capacity the members met, as was customary, in the Executive Council room in Government House; when sitting in its legislative capacity the members, minus Barton who was neither an elected nor an appointed member of that body, sat in the legislature in the Council Chamber of the Town Hall building. If committee business was being discussed, for example the standing finance committee under John's chairmanship which was obliged under the constitution to meet once a month, the meetings would take place in the Secretariat conference room. The arrangement was dispensed with after the elections to the Legisiative Council at the end of 1971, after which, as before, the Executive Council numbering seven including officials and a Legislative Council numbering nine including officials, would meet separately.

The members of the 1969 Legislative Council who sat as extraordinary members of Executive Council under the arrangement described above were W. H. Clement, nominated member of Legislative Council and ex-farm manager, Mrs Nanette King, elected member for Stanley and wife of the proprietor of the Upland Goose Hotel, and R. W. Hills, nominated member and successful local businessman.

The 1969 Legislative Council consisted of:

Sir Cosmo Haskard	President	
J. A. Jones	Colonial Secretary	senior member
L. C. Gleadell	Colonial Treasurer	member
R. V. Goss	elected member for Stanley	
R. M. Pitaluga	elected member for East Falkland	
S. Miller	elected member for West Falkland	
Mrs N. King	elected member for Stanley	
R. W. Hills	nominated member	
W. H. Clement	nominated member	

Mr Lewis had in the meantime taken over as Governor in January 1971.

In the elections for the Legislative Council, which took place towards the end of 1971, the results were as follows: L. G. Blake was elected unopposed as member for West Falkland; A. Monk was elected member for East Falkland – both are farm managers; S. Miller was elected member for Stanley; and W. E. Bowles, self employed in the carpentry and building business, was elected member for Stanley.

In the contest for the East Falkland seat one of the four sons of S. Miller was Monk's opponent. Monk won the contest by a decisive margin. In Stanley four candidates stood, two of them women. Of the two female candidates one was the sitting member, Mrs N. King. Their defeat by no very great margin indicated that they had split the pro-female vote between them.

The Governor nominated R. M. Pitaluga and W. B. Luxton, a farm manager in West Falkland, to the Legislative Council, thus making the composition of the 1971 Legislative Council as follows:

E. G. Lewis	President	
J. A. Jones	Colonial Secretary	senior member
L. C. Gleadell	Colonial Treasurer	member
S. Miller	elected member for Stanley	
L. G. Blake	elected member for West Falkland	
A. Monk	elected member for East Falkland	
W. E. Bowles	elected member for Stanley	
R. M. Pitaluga	nominated member	
W. B. Luxton	nominated member	

Goss, who took part in the first two rounds of talks with Argentina; Pitaluga, who took part in the first round; and R. W. Hills, who took part in the second round, did not stand in the election while Hills, who took part in the second round of talks, which resulted in the joint statement (agreement) of Buenos Aires of 1 July 1971, was not nominated to the Legislative Council again.

In the legislature the Colonial Secretary performs the role of leader of government business. The fact that the Governor nominates some members should not be taken to indicate that they toe a 'government line'. They are and always have been fiercely independent.

It will be clear from this description that the composition of the Executive Council cannot readily be decided until elections to the Legislative Council have taken place. For this reason, appointments to the Executive Council were made in mid-January 1972. The composition was then as follows:

E. G. Lewis	Chairman	
J. A. Jones	Colonial Secretary	senior member
L. C. Gleadell	Colonial Treasurer	member
S. Miller	elected member	
L. G. Blake	elected member	
A. G. Barton	appointed member	
A. Sloggie	appointed member	

This meant that, with the premature retirement of Gleadell from the service early in 1972 and the conclusion of John's tour of duty at the end of March of the same year, a new team would be dealing with 'the problem'. However, by this time the achievement of the initial breakthrough and the laying of solid ground work had already been accomplished. The rest of the task should be one of building upon this solid and hard won foundation.

These December elections were originally planned to take place in March 1972, but were brought forward so as not to clash with another round of talks expected to be be held in Stanley at approximately that time. John was expecting to wind up his three-year tour of duty on its conclusion. When we left the colony the date of round three was still uncertain. With telegrams flying and rumours naming April as a possibility circulating from Buenos Aires and London, I left a suitcase of useful odds and ends care of Mrs Heathman in the event of John being recalled at short notice from Buenos Aires. In any event, this round of talks slipped for an indefinite period and did not take place until November 1972, when the temporary airstrip opened. At these elections I voted for the first time in my life, for this was the only time I had been long enough in one place to be qualified to do so.

The new 'parliament' brought quite a few changes, but with elder statesmen Sidney Miller and A. G. Barton still in their seats, gerontocracy continued to be the order of the day. Sidney, an irascible ex-farm manager, was nicknamed 'the hangman' because of the strong stand he took when the question of hanging was debated in the legislature following Britain's final abolition of the death penalty. AGB, as he was popularly known, is reputed to be the wealthiest man in the colony. It was an interesting election with quite a number of surprises, one of which was the appointment of the Colonial Manager of the Falkland Islands Company as a member of the Executive Council. It was some time since the company's manager had sat on this body. Another unexpected turn was what many islanders considered to be the over representation of farm managers and the new 'parliament' was soon dubbed 'the cowboy administration'.

The first round of talks on communications had been entirely exploratory. In the course of it the Argentine side made a number of offers, including one to construct an airfield and operate an air service between the colony and the Argentine mainland. These talks were confidential and, with 1968 in mind, the islanders were suspicious that secret agreements had been reached in London behind their backs. Members of the Executive and Legislative Councils knew that this was not the case, but their lips were sealed and an uneasy period followed during which the authorities in the colony pressed for publication of the content of the talks.

The timing of the announcement by the Falkland Islands Company that the *Darwin* would be withdrawn from service at the end of 1971, thus severing the colony's passenger link with the South American mainland, did nothing to allay the already mounting tensions. The islanders had, by the usual progression of one step forward two steps back, succeeded in convincing themselves that they were about to be sold down the river. Under these circumstances, an agreement was reached to release information on the content of the talks and it became possible for the islanders to be taken into the government's confidence and, in turn, for the government to sound out the islanders' opinion. As a result a more relaxed atmosphere prevailed, thus paving the way for a softening of attitudes and to preparing the groundwork for the next round.

During most of this difficult period John was in charge of the colony's affairs. No one was more aware than he of the urgent need to take the islanders into confidence about the ground covered in the first round of talks, but understandably the powers that be were not prepared to move on until the new Governor had had the time and opportunity to assess the situation for himself. Consequently, John had to bear the brunt of local suspicion during the interregnum.

Governor Haskard's additional year in office had expired in September 1970. In between the last bouts of entertaining, Lady Haskard packed hectically, often in the small hours of the morning, and the corridors of power at Government House became a hazardous steeplechase of trunks and packing cases. The sad day of departure dawned. *Darwin*, dressed overall, with passengers already aboard, lay off in mid-harbour ready to receive the Governor while the populace turned up at the corner of Ross Road by the Public jetty to see them off. Leading personalities and their wives waited at the end of the windy jetty, in strict order of seniority, to receive the final gubernatorial handshake prior to the ship's departure. Marines in parade dress lined the jetty. The Government House taxi arrived with Lieutenant-Commander Tony Peebles, commanding officer of the hovercraft unit, in attendance, and the Governor, resplendent in full uniform, alighted to be greeted by John. We accompanied them past the groups of wellwishers, along the Public jetty to inspect the guard of honour. The last farewells were said and the Governor and his wife boarded MV *Forrest* for the short trip to where the *Darwin* was lying off.

Once the Governor and his party were aboard the *Darwin*, the colourful ceremony proceeded with the ship first sailing in a westerly direction towards the Head of the Bay before turning to sail in an easterly direction past the town of Stanley, while gun salutes were fired from the shore and acknowledged by His Excellency at the salute on the wing of the ship's bridge.

The moving farewell did not take place without one incident of light relief. Shortly after the *Darwin* had disappeared through the Narrows, it was noticed with some curiosity, that MV *Forrest* steamed back to the Public jetty at great speed, then departed with equal rapidity through the Narrows, and then back again to tie up at its usual place. It transpired that in the last minute flurry of farewells the Governor's briefcase, which contained all the work he intended to do on the four-and-a-half day trip to Montevideo, had been left behind and the *Darwin* had to hang fire in Port William while the *Forrest*, under the urgings of Tony Peebles, collected the offending item.

The interregnum was to last until the middle of January. This turned out to be a hectic period with the beginning of the season thrown in for good measure. Tony and Lynn Peebles came to stay with us for a week while they packed their belongings, and Stan and I were fascinated to see with what naval precision they carried out their morning breakfast routine. Lynn, an ex-Wren meteorological officer, had come out on the *AES* to join her husband and had taken over from the eccentric Scots government forecaster Danny Borland when he went on leave. Lynn gained such a reputation for her accurate forecasts that Danny had to look to his laurels on his return.

Bishop Tucker from Buenos Aires, within whose diocese the colony falls, arrived for a short stay and was entertained at Sulivan House. The colony had been without a padre since the end of June and the bishop's visit was to be followed by that of Canon Wilcockson and his wife from Rio de Janeiro, to help fill the gap over the Christmas period.

An amusing anecdote is told about an earlier bishop who was astute enough to turn the Argentine claim to his advantage. On his return to Buenos Aires from visiting the colony he refused to allow customs officials to examine his baggage on the grounds that he had been travelling internally in Argentina. The officials were compelled to agree. We were later able to cap this story as when we visited a *cambio* in Buenos Aires in the hope of buying some Chilean escudos for the next leg of our South American journey, we were informed that only nationals of the countries bordering Chile could do so. They were hoist with their own petard when we produced our travel documents, agreed upon in the 1971 round of talks in Buenos Aires, and flashed them, like FBI agents, before their startled eyes. They could not argue their way out of that one either and good humouredly gave way, thus enabling us to eke out the miserable rate of exchange forced upon visitors to Chile who do not have the good fortune to be born in Argentina, Bolivia or Peru.

During the interregnum, the steady flow of cipher traffic became a deluge. This was a three-way operation between the Falkland Islands, London and Buenos Aires, with the islands at the apex and bearing the strain because the other two had the advantage of mechanical equipment, while in Stanley the entire task had to be carried out by hand. Saturday morning was a favourite time for the arrival of the latest batch of messages, the Foreign and Commonwealth Office obviously clearing its desks in anticipation of a free weekend. However, we were occasionally able to return a salvo on a Saturday afternoon which perhaps entailed some dismay at the other end.

In addition to the usual social round inseparable from the beginning of the season, parades, bazaars, school prizegivings, and Christmas race meetings were once more upon us. With Government House in the throes of a facelift in preparation for the arrival of the new Governor, and Government House staff leave having also to be fitted into the interregnum, Sulivan House took over as the setting for cocktail parties. Whenever I had a spare moment I would dart round Government House to inspect progress and on one such foray I discovered that the original stock of pillows was still in use. An urgent request was sent through BAS channels for two dozen replacement pillows to be put on board the *Bransfield*.

During this hectic period, a team chosen by Governor Haskard visited Argentina on a fact-finding economic mission. Its members, whom we saw off on the *Darwin*, were the Colonial Treasurer Les Gleadell, the master of RMS *Darwin* Nigel Miller, both of whom were islanders, and A. Sloggie, the Colonial Manager of the Falkland Islands Company whose wife was a Falkland Islander. All three were understandably apprehensive at the prospect of this journey into the unknown, but John was able to reassure them that Sir Michael Hadow, the ambassador, and his staff at Buenos Aires would take care of them. For Sloggie and Miller, with the company's future trading policy uncertain, the visit presented both difficulties and opportunities, while for Les Gleadell, the problem was more personal as his firm handling of the DC6 hijack incident a few years earlier had, at the instigation of the leader of the Condor group, made him the subject of legal action in the Argentine courts. Although Les was aware of the possibility of harassment, he recognised the importance of the mission to the colony and we admired his determination to lead it.

In fact, while the three men were visiting Argentine ports to assess their suitability for trading purposes with the colony, the Condor leader seized the opportunity to reopen the legal charge he had brought against Gleadell, and this naturally disrupted the smooth running of their itinerary. The incident attracted headline coverage in newspapers throughout Argentina and was featured on the BBC's programme Radio Newsreel. Despite intense diplomatic activity, a shadow had once again been cast over the prospects for rapprochement, though in retrospect, however, the effects of this incident turned out to be less serious than had been feared and Gleadell took it all in his stride. Even if their mission had served to harden existing economic positions, it had at least done no harm to diplomatic relations.

Some time later, Owens, the manager of the Newest Store, visited Argentina and it was noticeable that, shortly after his return, a greatly increased variety of goods at very competitive prices appeared on the shelves of the West store. One party was over, but perhaps another was just beginning.

Chapter 13
The Quality of Mercy

Mid-January saw the arrival by HMS *Endurance* from Punta Arenas of Mr Lewis the Governor designate, a former acquaintance of John's from Nigeria days. Despite better relations with Argentina it was still deemed wiser at that time for the new Governor to avoid Buenos Aires – hence the roundabout route organised via Santiago and Punta Arenas. Mr Lewis's arrival coincided with the news of the kidnapping of the British ambassador in Montevideo, so I imagine the Foreign and Commonwealth Office breathed a sigh of relief that he had not come on the *Darwin*.

The swearing-in ceremony took place in the Council Chamber with the Governor-Designate and Acting Governor arriving from Sulivan House. As his uniform had not yet arrived the new Governor wore morning dress. Among the elite of the colony invited to the ceremony was Captain Rodney Bowden of HMS *Endurance*, along with a member from each deck of the ship. As was customary, past and present members of the Executive and Legislative Councils (and retired farm managers) attended. For this occasion the Council Chamber was filled to capacity, in contrast with the usual meagre turnout when the legislature was sitting. In the corridor outside, the broadcasting unit had set up its equipment and was making last-minute tests and adjustments; Terry Peck, the Inspector of Police, was ready to announce the Governor-Designate and the audience was looking expectant' when at the very last minute, the clerk of the council, Nap Bound, rushed into the chamber bearing a glass of water, which he placed on the dais in full view of the interested spectators. A message had been relayed that Mr Lewis would require a drink. The liquid was extremely cloudy and, as I watched the sediment slowly settle to the bottom of the glass, my mind wandered from the solemnity of the occasion and I speculated on its peat content and flavour. Needless to say it remained untouched.

With the swearing in completed, John made a brief speech to welcome the new Governor, to which Mr Lewis replied, and the local notables lined up to be introduced, after which we accompanied Mr Lewis to Government House to introduce him to his staff and new domain. Later that evening a cocktail party was held at Sulivan House to enable members of the Executive and Legislative Councils and their wives to meet the new boss.

During the waiting period, while the new Governor was settling in and getting the feel of things, I must confess to a feeling of reluctance at relinquishing the premier role. It had been an intensely interesting, hard-working and rewarding time and the experience of handling the colony's affairs for an extended period had proved what I had previously suspected, that the Falkland Islands is too small a scene for both a Governor and a Colonial Secretary.

As seasonal visitors came and went on *Bransfield* and *Endurance*, the period of comparative calm continued. Shipping activity included a growing number of Russian fishing vessels, which perhaps gave rise to material published in a British newspaper that Russia was engaged in trade with the colony. The successful visit of Colonel Huarte further contributed to the unruffled tempo of life.

This quiet period came to an abrupt end with the McMullen affair. During the first round of talks in London in 1970 the Argentines had made a without any strings offer, to send in an Argentine air force amphibian aircraft, normally used for air/sea rescue operations, in the event of a medical emergency. The islands' medical authorities had been told about the offer, but the general public did not yet known about it. Just such an emergency arose when McMullen, one of the lighthouse keepers, suffered a severe internal haemorrhage.

Whenever an incident of this kind occurs in the islands it brings out the best in the islands character and everyone pulls together in a concerted effort. The Hovercraft Unit was alerted and flew out to the lighthouse and over the terrain, while the Beaver went to investigate the possibility of landing nearby, but both the site and weather conditions made this impossible. Evacuation by Land Rover was not contemplated as the jolting might have proved fatal, so it fell to the navy to bring the patient into hospital. After a period during which calls for blood donors were answered by the few Marines and Stanley residents who had the correct blood group, it was decided, with the agreement of members of council, to put the Argentine mercy flight offer to the test, as the patient's chances were minimal.

Telegrams were exchanged and arrangements made for the flight. The Colonial Secretary planned the operations and, with none of the normal infrastructure available for this sort of exercise, coordinated the islands' genius for improvisation. Police and Public Works Department employees were posted along the sea wall; Jim Kerr, the director of FIGAS, with Chilean-born and Spanish-speaking Joe Booth of the Falkland Islands Company accompanying him as interpreter, flew out to lead in the Albatross amphibian. Joe Booth's daughter Miriam manned the airlines office radio telephone, and Ian Campbell, the other pilot, was ready at the FIGAS hangar to take off in the second 'Beaver' should the need arise.

Stanley wireless station was alerted to play its part and Danny the Met did overtime. Ted Clapp, of the BAS, and his boys were ready in a marine tender with firefighting equipment; various launches were arranged to bring doctors and crew ashore. Ian Strange's Zodiac was to go alongside the Albatross to act as a bridge between it and the launch in the tricky operation of conveying the patient from launch to plane. The Hovercraft Unit was at standby and All-Stanley, in a line of Land Rovers stretching from near the hangar for more than half a mile back beyond Government House, was out to witness the early arrival of the amphibian.

At about 9.30 a.m. the lumbering aircraft loomed out of misty low-lying cloud and landed in a sheet of spray, with what seemed to inexperienced onlookers a terrifying juddering stop, on the other side of the harbour opposite Sulivan House. It was the first friendly Argentine plane to arrive in the colony and I felt it appropriate that it should be an Albatross that surmounted the barrier to the 'Islas de Soledad'. Such an idea would have appealed to the romantic soul of the writer whose nostalgic poem picturing the islands as accessible only to the penguins and the albatross had appeared in an Argentine magazine supplement.

After a conference in the hospital between Argentine and island medical authorities, it was decided, despite the rapidly deteriorating weather conditions, to go ahead with the lift out, which was successfully achieved in the early afternoon. News was received the same evening over the ham radio network of the patient's safe arrival in the British hospital in Buenos Aires.

This incident appealed to the popular imagination in the colony and in Argentina and created an atmosphere of goodwill on both sides. In spite of the fact that the patient died, not unexpectedly, in the British hospital, the Argentine government's quick response to the Falkland Islands government's plea did much to soften attitudes. It had brought a breakthrough in Falkland Islands–Argentine relations.

Chapter 14
Of Shoes and Ships

The *Darwin* sailing of mid-March brought Mrs Lewis, the Governor's wife, and Elizabeth Ogilvie, Third Secretary in the British embassy in Buenos Aires. Argentina was her first posting in the diplomatic service and she had been finding the change of scene and climate in Buenos Aires rather trying; like my journey in reverse, it was to prove a welcome and beneficial break for her. John was pleased at the arrival of a third female passenger, Audrey Gann, sent out under British Technical Assistance as secretarial instructor.

Elizabeth stayed with us at Sulivan House and wasted no time getting to know Stanley and its inhabitants before we set off on *Darwin* round the islands. A *Darwin* camp trip is not to be compared with the aching discomfort of the Stanley–Montevideo express, as stops at the small isolated settlements are frequent and most of the steaming is done at night in reasonably sheltered inland waters, thus the ship's movement is much less noticeable, except in certain notorious stretches such as the Cape Dolphin area and the Tamar Rapids, when I lay back, sedated as usual with Avomine. There are usually few passengers doing the round trip, which gives rise to the luxurious impression of travelling in one's own private yacht, particularly if able to enjoy the civilisation of the owner's cabin.

This impression was heightened on this occasion by the fact that we were a mere handful of passengers, a pleasant, polyglot group of expatriates. In addition to Elizabeth and myself, there were Meg Layer, a South African librarian engaged in research for her bibliography, Mr Larssen, the Swedish SAS representative from Montevideo, and the youngest member of the Joint Services Satellite Tracking Team, on a working trip. This team, which was based in Stanley for a few months, took over a house belonging to a European space research organisation and its members were soon competing with each other to produce interesting mutton delicacies garnished with vegetables from the Sulivan House garden. Our large garden produced too much for our requirements, but it did enable us to keep short-term visitors well supplied.

As camp trips were very much working affairs entailing delivering stores and collecting bales of wool from the settlements for later shipment from Stanley by the *AES* for auction in Britain, a relaxed atmosphere prevailed on board. Meals were informal occasions with passengers usually remaining comfortably clad in slacks, sweaters, thick socks and Wellingtons throughout the trip, anoraks at the ready for jaunts ashore.

Gumboots are the norm in camp because you encounter mud as soon as you step off the jetty, from where there are only rough tracks leading to the settlements. The usual practice for visitors is to remove gumboots in the porch by the front door of a house and pad about in stockinged soles – hence the usefulness of the thick fishermen's socks always worn. The normal method of transport from jetty to farm house is by Land Rover, even if only a few hundred yards away, and the frenzied barking of sheepdogs, which seem on occasion to be more numerous than the human population, always greets one's approach to the farm settlement.

Each shepherd will own half a dozen or more sheepdogs, necessary for his work. These working dogs stay outside, which is probably why the incidence of hydatid disease turned out to be lower than expected in the camp. Perhaps because of their innate conservatism, however, many shepherds needed a lot of convincing before they could be persuaded of the effectiveness of Scolaban in breaking the cycle of the disease. On some farms the shepherds believed that the best worm dose for dogs was gunpowder, which they obtained from shotgun cartridges.

Most settlements are built near wooden jetties with the woolshed close by so that the bales can be loaded straight from shed to scow for transport to *Darwin* or *AES*. The first impression one has of a settlement is aghast amazement at its smallness and drab isolation. No amount of reading nor photographs can quite prepare one for the shock of actually witnessing the solitude endured by these tiny communities amidst their desolate surroundings. Conditions are less primitive than they once were, but old style lavatories still exist as reminders of those days when the loos were built directly over a stream which provided a natural flush below.

Settlements, though tiny, consisting of the farm manager's house, the cookhouse for the bachelors with a resident cook to look after them and seldom more than half a dozen cottages, are self-contained units, each household baking its own bread, churning butter, milking the cow and feeding the hens while the men work long hours on low wages droving, dipping, shearing, fencing and doing general maintenance work around the farms. On the other hand, comfortable, modern dwellings are provided, often with central heating installed.

Cattle are killed in winter for consumption and each household has its share while hoggets are culled whenever the larder is empty. Farm workers have a generous allowance of free food and milk. As in Stanley, they grow their own vegetables, quite often with better results and camp potatoes are popular in the capital. Natural spring water is an added advantage. Peat, which is practically on the doorstep, is cut on a communal basis and the farm settlement generator provides electricity for a fixed period each evening.

By the same token, farm managers' salaries are compensated by good housing. Standards vary, but these houses are often large and quite luxurious and they do get generous paid leave. Household provisions and commodities are obtained from the company store, run usually by the foreman, sometimes by the manager if the settlement is particularly small, or in a few cases by a storeman/bookkeeper. The cost of purchases is deducted from the employee's wages, consequently in the camp there is not much occasion for handling money. To illustrate this point, not so long ago at Green Patch the manager, who also ran the store, was short of change. One of the settlement wives came to the rescue saying, 'I have got some in a vase'. She produced it and, on tipping the vase up, out fell several gold sovereigns. The money had probably not been touched for years.

A camp trip always entailed a clamber whether *Darwin* was alongside at the few settlements where the water is deep enough to allow a ship to tie up, or laying off, necessitating a trip ashore by launch or scow. Slacks were the only possible wear for the undignified scramble at low tide up an endlessly long rickety ladder onto a wooden jetty, or a push and heave from the launch to shore, or over and among sheep on *Darwin*'s deck, or down a ladder after climbing over dozens of oil drums to reach the ship's side. A certain amount of agility as well as old clothing was absolutely essential, as was a sense of humour. However, the famous Falkland Islands' hospitality for which the camp is particularly noted and the tonic effect on one's lungs of so much fresh air, made it well worth the effort entailed.

I had been told that camp air was purer, and it did surprisingly seem to be the case, but it could also be colder as the countryside is more open and consequently more exposed to the winds. One had only to consider the searing effect on the grass to realise what the wind could do to the complexion. The combination of sun and wind can burn and in that southern climate the strength of the ultra violet rays out of a cloudless sky could, because of the cooling effect of the wind, catch you unawares. A more disastrous effect of the wind can sometimes be seen in elderly shepherds suffering permanent loss of muscle control under the eyes, which remain permanently open.

Our trip round the islands was to take in most of the settlements on East Falkland. Once more we sailed through the Narrows and into Berkeley Sound to spend the afternoon on deck in the glass-sided shelter, alternately admiring or despairing at the rocky scenery and the desolation of the bare windswept moorland. From the geological formation of the rocks, it was apparent why the Marines' rock climbing experts found them too crumbly to attempt. It seemed uncanny to sail for hours and see nothing on land – no trees, no bushes, not even sheep, only the accompanying escort of black and white shags, their necks outstretched and heads swivelling.

Our first stop was at Green Patch in a howling gale and driving rain squalls where we did not bother to venture ashore, contenting ourselves with watching the clouds scud across the lowering skies and the wind whipping up the waves. From there it was a short sailing distance to Port Louis on the opposite side of the Sound, arriving in time for the evening meal to be taken while the ship was at anchor.

By this time the wind had dropped and, immediately after the meal, we went ashore in the gathering dusk. I had been nursing a large enamel teapot all the way from Stanley to deliver to Jenny, Mr and Mrs Heathman's daughter, whose husband had left the police force to return to the land. Before her father's retirement from the camp, Jenny had joined him shepherding. Like all campers who distrust the bright lights of Stanley for any length of time, she was glad to be back to the isolation.

Jenny showed us over her Port Louis home, the original stone building Louis Vernet and his family had occupied and later used by that the British as the seat of government until Governor Moody (1842–48) assumed office and Lord Stanley reached an agreement with the naval authorities to move the headquarters to Port William. The attractive stone building with its incredibly thick walls and mullioned windows overlooking the inlet is now a farm settlement occupied by two families, though some consider that a building of such historical interest should be preserved as a museum.

Fittingly, we made the trip by moonlight in Jenny's Land Rover to the small cemetery, where the graves of Bourgainville's settlers and members of the crew of *Erebus* lie hidden among overgrown, coarse, tussacy grass and, to the amazement of some nearby sheep, we groped our way in the fitful light among the fallen headstones. Abandoning our attempt to locate all the graves in the moonlight, Jenny drove us back to the jetty and we admired the agility with which she sprang out to open and close each gate. We climbed over the heavily laden scows and into the launch for the trip back to the *Darwin*. It was a memorable scene – the dark still water of the inlet reflecting the dim light from the shore, the moon creating a path of gold to the gleaming lights of *Darwin* ahead, the outlines of the scows tied together being towed behind the launch, the men standing on the bales, their faces lit momentarily by the glow from a cigarette, and our slow stately procession back to our floating hotel.

Early next morning we awoke to find ourselves at Johnson's Harbour. Work in camp begins very early, particularly at that time of the year when the men have already put in almost a full day's work before breakfast at eight o'clock. Elizabeth and I had been told that if we wanted to go ashore we should be ready by seven. We staggered out of our bunks only to find that as no one had reminded us about the one hour's difference between camp and Stanley time in summer, we had been caught: we were up an hour too soon, but, as so often is the case in the islands, it was the best time of the day before the wind got up and we sat on deck basking in the bright sunshine. By eight o'clock the day had turned grey and cold and on our return from shore to ship we had to crouch under the prow of the launch to dodge a heavy rain squall.

Once ashore we were met by the farm manager, Mr Smith, who showed us over the small, neat settlement. The grass in settlements is always much smoother and greener than elsewhere, presumably because of the regular manuring from grazing animals, and walking was a pleasure instead of having to keep a watchful eye on uneven ankle twisting patches. We were then taken to the farmhouse where tea and cakes were produced. This was smoko for them, but for us it was breakfast. Mr Smith showed us over the company store, a feature of each settlement, usually well stocked with stores to a value of several thousand pounds. This store was particularly fascinating with its solid wooden counters and shelves packed with goods, including a fine collection of kerosene lamps and packets of maté tea. Other treasures were a beautifully finished leather side-saddle, which had belonged to the manager's grandmother, lovingly polished to a satiny texture which was a joy to touch, and a type of spit used by old-time settlers, which consisted of a central shaft from which hung half a dozen hooks for cooking over an open fireplace.

The South American influence in the islands is exemplified by the drinking of maté tea, which is more prevalent in the camp, but even so hardly widespread. Some of the older shepherds have adopted the habit of brewing the green leaves of the yerba tree. This is drunk from a maté gourd which, when first used, has to be seasoned in a ritualistic way. First, the maté leaves are put in the gourd and then boiling water is poured over them. It is left for some time to impregnate the gourd. This process is repeated several times until the gourd is considered ready for use. To prepare the tea, boiling water is poured over a thick bed of the leaves to which sugar is added if desired. The resultant brew is then siphoned up through an intricately and delicately engraved metal tube called a *bombilla*. When we left the islands I handed over a spare maté gourd and *bombilla*, along with a large packet of yerba tea, to a delighted Pongo, an inmate of the old people's section in the King Edward Memorial Hospital. There is a saying that once you have drunk maté tea you will always return to South America. I became more addicted to it than John, so we shall see!

Other ways in which South American influence is noticeable, especially in the camp, is the terminology for blood stock and horse gear. For example, the corrupt Spanish terms '*preto*' and '*pinto*' are used for 'black' and 'piebald'. Sheepskins are flung over a high saddle in gaucho fashion and intricate handmade horse gear is in use dating from the times of the gauchos . The dress adopted by many campers is in the gaucho style, as is the sideways manner of riding, with one hand on the reins leaving the other free to switch the horse's rump or roll a cigarette, a trick of which they are proud and at which they are adept. This sideways seat possibly evolved from the need to keep a watch on the sheep or to evade the force of the wind. Horses receive little attention, are seldom rubbed down, and go unshod.

At the entrance to all farm settlements is a barred iron grid, like the British cattle grid but known by its Spanish name, *paseo libre*. The remains of the old gaucho corrals can still be seen and are conspicuous when you fly over the camp. The names of settlements such as Salvador, San Carlos and Rincon Grande indicate their Spanish influence; the *bola*s are still used in the camp to catch Upland geese, with cattle and sheep knuckle bones being used for the balls. A term of affection is '*che*' and 'cheers *che*' is the customary island farewell. The word 'camp' itself is derived from the Spanish.

Before we returned to *Darwin* we were shown over the woolshed, which led directly onto the jetty and we inspected the machinery used for baling and banding and the special soft quality for which Falkland Islands wool is noted. There is a camp custom, in the woolsheds, not applicable to women, that when a stranger visits for the first time his 'shoes are chalked', which means that a chalk circle is drawn on the floor round his feet. To break the circle a fine is levied, in liquor, usually a bottle of rum.

The same afternoon on arrival at Salvador, a model farm, we were invited to tea by owner and manager Robin Pitaluga and his wife Gene, a London girl who has settled down splendidly to life in camp, baking, butter-making and coping with visitors galore. She gave us a splendid tea and had obviously indulged in a mad baking session in honour of our arrival. Not many children have a naval helicopter as a playroom, but their two small sons do, almost at the door. This was the result of engine failure in one of HMS *Endurance*'s helicopters which came down in Salvador waters. Despite being towed ashore by Robin Pitaluga, it was found not to be worth salvaging.

Suffering from a surfeit of cream cakes – and we were only halfway through the camp trip – we staggered aboard again and sailed to our next port of call, Teal Inlet, where the manager, David Barton, had invited us ashore for dinner. It was pitch dark by the time we landed and we made our way by Land Rover in inky blackness to what seemed a deserted settlement. There we were treated to a gourmet meal prepared by Mrs Barton, Robin Pitaluga's sister, of – guess what? – saddle of lamb, but compensated for me by fresh raspberries from the garden and, of course, the inevitable farmhouse cream. Such rich camp fare was already, I was sure, taking its toll of both liver and figure and I could now understand why visitors to camp returned to Stanley looking pounds heavier.

The next afternoon saw us at Pebble Island, which had a more spacious, exhilerating feel after the hemmed in atmosphere of inland waters. Situated off the north coast of West Falkland where it enjoys the full benefit of bracing sea winds, Pebble Island is one of the more picturesque of the myriad islands which make up the colony with its range of hills in the distance, the fresh saltiness of the open sea, the long stretches of silver sands and a piratical looking hulk in the small harbour.

We had arrived in a gale and work was held up for several hours as it was too rough to work the scows. *Darwin* camp schedules can never be adhered to as loading and unloading can be held up for hours, even days, while waiting for the weather to moderate. Luckily, by late afternoon the gale had abated somewhat and we were able to go ashore in a force five wind. At the jetty we encountered such a swell that the heaving-off party waiting there took one horrified look at the three female passengers and made a no-go sign. I must admit I had been eyeing the heaving launch and long ladder with some trepidation and was relieved when we were taken round in the lee of the jetty to beach the launch. For once we were able to enjoy a walk up to the settlement instead of having to climb into the ubiquitous Land Rover.

Mrs Evans, the farm manager's wife, gave us directions to the sandy beach and we walked into the glow of a setting sun, the sky flushed with pink-tipped clouds, across the tussacy ground, past the peat bogs, accompanied by the cat, to look for pebbles for which the island is noted. The smooth stones make attractive jewellery and even the unpolished pebbles make a pleasant eye-catching collection. The usual flotilla of young logger ducks took no notice of the intruders striding along the sandy beach in the stinging wind. We returned to a roaring fire in an attractively designed fireplace of red brick, the grate set at almost waist height, and a dinner of the usual rich camp fare.

Next day's sailing took us up the Falkland Sound past Ajax Bay and its abandoned freezing plant, another relic of Labour's great days of grandiose overseas schemes. This was the Falklands' groundnut scheme. We steamed on into deteriorating weather of heavy rain squalls and spray lashing the decks and portholes, past wild, desolate wastes of uninhabited countryside. The rock formations here were strange, nightmarish almost, the haunt of cormorants and shags which escorted us through the Tamar Rapids where cross currents met and the tiderip pulled.

By next morning we were tied up to the jetty in the calm waters of Port Howard, one of the few settlements with a deep water harbour. Mr and Mrs Pole-Evans, the first Falkland Islanders John and I had met at the Colombia Palace Hotel on our way south through Montevideo, had invited us for breakfast. The usual ritual of removing boots was followed by a gay breakfast party, the table groaning with farm produce, after which we set off for a walk round the settlement to work off its effect. This farm, which belongs to

Waldrons, is the best kept in the colony. Enlightened ownership has ensured that profits have been ploughed back into the land and experiments carried out. It is also one of the few settlements with a population large enough to merit having a settlement school with its own resident schoolmaster.

Set in a hollow enclosed entirely by hills, Port Howard, I felt, was a damp, dark, depressing place with rain never far away. We had only gone a few hundred yards of our walk when the hint of a drizzle turned into a downpour, which continued throughout the morning transforming the tracks to a sea of mud. We tramped on, increasingly sodden, looking for footholds in the squelching mire. Back at the settlement we were shown over the enormous woolsheds and haylofts where the traditional Two Nighters were held and the stable below with its fine collection of horsegear, but by then, I must confess, I was so miserably wet that I had lost interest and abandoned the rest of our party to return to the *Darwin* for a hot bath and a treble medicinal brandy.

A few hours sailing took us to San Carlos by mid-afternoon where we encountered gale force winds and an ominously oppressive sky. Unloading was again postponed as the seas were too rough to lower the scows. In response to an invitation to tea from Mr and Mrs Monk, Captain Miller took the passengers off in the launch, but as I had not recovered from my morning soaking I elected to stay on board where I had an amusing insight into camp gossip as I listened in to the radio telephone network with Radio Edith in Stanley at the centre and various settlement wives tuning in. The weather continued to deteriorate and as there was no hope of being able to unload that evening, the Monks had their guests for dinner as well. To afford some relaxation for the crew, an ancient Norman Wisdom film was shown in the lounge, which provided suitable light relief in those surroundings. A good belly laugh helped me to recover my equilibrium.

Next morning Elizabeth left us to spend the night at Fox Bay West. Through mutual friends in Buenos Aires, the Robertsons had extended an invitation and arrangements were made through the Colonial Secretary for her to transfer from *Darwin* to one of the Beavers. In perfect weather the bright flash of the scarlet Beaver appeared out of a clear blue sky, buzzing us as *Darwin* dropped anchor, before landing a short distance away, whereupon Elizabeth grabbed her case and was transferred the few yards by motor launch, to be whisked off by Ian Campbell.

After that spot of excitement we continued round the curve of the next headland to Port San Carlos, where Mr Miller, Nigel Miller's brother, was on the jetty to meet us with his two small daughters and to transport us by Land Rover up the track to the settlement. KC, as it is known, owned by the Cameron family, where Stan had spent many years shepherding, is a charming rambling residence with a garden sheltering inside a peat dyke. After a gargantuan lunch laid on by the manager's wife whose hobby was cooking, we returned to the jetty to find that our fellow passengers for the rest of the journey had beaten us to it and were already on board,taking up so much room on the foredeck, our normal mode of boarding on camp trips where the sheep have priority, that there was nothing for it but to take a deep breath before literally clambering over their backs, clinging precariously to projecting bits of the ship along a narrow rubber hose attached to the side of the bridge. The exercise helped to digest the inevitable lashings of cream which accompany all camp meals, but the sharp, acrid smell of sheep had the contrary effect. Return from a camp trip necessitates the immediate immersion of self and all clothing

14. The *Darwin* leaving Port San Carlos.

in the wash tub to rid one's nostrils of the penetrating, lingering smell of sheep.

And so, from there we left with a full cargo, via Cape Dolphin on the last leg back to Stanley, to arrive very early the next morning just in time to see the HMS *Endurance* getting up steam to depart through the Narrows .

Towards the end of our tour John managed to snatch a few days local leave and we embarked on the last camp trip to be made in *Darwin* with Nigel Miller as captain. It was to be a short three-day trip, but it was cut even shorter as Nigel had to finish packing up his household effects before taking the ship for the last time as master to Montevideo, there to hand over to Ken Archibald, on loan from the Liverpool Port Authority. Ken was an ex-BAS ship's officer and knew the islands and *Darwin* well, having acted as relief master once before. He was a popular figure, albeit with some big ship eccentricities, such as heralding the ship's arrival and departure by playing music over the loud speaker system.

On this camp trip we called at Goose Green, the largest settlement in the islands with a population of approximately 100 and the appearance of a small village. This is the location of the Falkland Islands Company's camp manager. It has the distinction of possessing the world s largest woolshed. At one time Goose Green brought employment to the islands with the export of canned meat, but this venture came to an end during the First World War. A revival of the frozen meat industry at Ajax Bay soon after the Second World War failed, this time owing to the shortage of suitable sheep.

We were awakened by the grinding of derricks at 5.00 a.m. and roused ourselves to go ashore to be shown over Darwin boarding school. In addition to inspecting the school and checking on maintenance and other needs, John was taking the opportunity to explain to the staff the implications of the Buenos Aires agreement and how it would affect their movements in and out of the colony on leave. After the usual oil-drum marathon necessary to disembark we walked the half mile or so along the springy grass, well manured by the large number of Upland Geese cropping away regardless of our presence.

Darwin boarding school is run for children in camp and is financed by the Falkland Islands government. The two-storey building, which some say was originally constructed by the Falkland Islands Company for its own needs, was donated by the company to the government for use as a school. Staff are recruited from Britain. Primary school subjects are taught up to age 11 or 12, at which stage a child can sit the scholarship exam, but few choose to continue their education in Britain or South America. Post primary subjects are taken between the ages of 12 and 15, the school leaving age. The recent emphasis of the curriculum is on the outward bound type of training, which sets the right sort of atmosphere for camp children, several of whom have entered the Duke of Edinburgh's award scheme. Consequently, outdoor pursuits such as canoeing, swimming and archery are becoming increasingly popular.

Children in camp, however, are at an educational disadvantage. If they live in isolated settlements, they are not obliged to attend school until the age of seven when they rely solely on the itinerant camp teacher for their education, an inadequate system as the camp teacher, who has perhaps five or six settlements to visit, spends a week or two at each settlement in turn on his rounds by Beaver. Homework is set but circumstances all too often lead to its being skimped. Camp parents have often not had the benefit of education and so do not see the need for it. Children who come in from camp to attend school in Stanley frequently find it difficult to catch up to the prevailing standards.

The island character is one of contrasts. Although often formally uneducated, campers in particular are not lacking in ingenuity, as the following anecdote indicates. A shepherd living near Volunteer Point who gave a visitor a lift back to Stanley in his ancient Land Rover was a wizard at improvisation. When his vehicle broke down on the way and he found that an essential part had dropped off, he simply cut the heel off his Wellington boot to make a thick washer, which saw them safely into town. Another story to illustrate the campers ingenuity concerns a shepherd's method of feeding his hens when he had to leave them for two to three weeks to go into the main settlement for shearing. He shot a bullock and left it where it lay so that the hens could help themselves! When one old workman who was nailing a corrugated iron roof on a shed in cold weather accidentally hammered a nail through his thumb because his fingers were numb and his sight poor, he merely extracted the nail with the claw of the hammer and carried on with the job.

There are many colourful camp characters and legendary tales, not printable here, have grown up round them. Some, like the Bertrands of Carcass Island, deliberately cultivate a reputation for eccentricity and the late Mr Davis of New Island was known as 'the pirate'. One character must of necessity remain anonymous, namely the gleaming white skeleton, complete with a set of ship's officer's brass buttons, which was discovered not so long ago at the top of a mountain.

Perhaps the naive unworldliness of camp character is epitomised by the elderly lady who was awarded a decoration in the New Year's Honours List. She considered that since she had earned it in camp that was the appropriate place to receive it. The Governor of the day arranged to call at a certain time to present the award on behalf of Her Majesty and the old lady was not at all pleased when HE was an hour late for the appointment, and she told him so in no uncertain terms. Another amusing story is recounted of the contraceptive pill which had been doled out to a family. When, to the doctor's surprise, the lady produced the usual bouncing nine-pounder, it transpired that it was the husband who had swallowed the pills. Their insularity, however, is not to be admired and I feel sorry for visitors, whose attitude to the local scene is coloured by the clannishness of the islands' attitudes and there have been regrettable instances when an incomer, willing to throw in a lot with the islanders, has been frozen out.

Oddly, many Stanley residents have never been to camp. I do not know whether the reverse is true, but I imagine it is unlikely if the flight schedules broadcast nightly are anything to go by. Perhaps their ideas about their camp cousins are as outdated and strange as those held by many Argentinians who envisage the islanders behaving like the gauchos of

Patagonia, drinking endless brews of maté. Camp cousins may be less sophisticated than their Stanley counterparts, but they enjoy the same foibles and weaknesses, the same failed marriages, good humoured scandals and legalised wife swapping. Reports of weddings, horse races, whist drives and other social functions relayed on The Box each Friday night sound alike; they are perhaps more prone to succumb to the demon drink, a fault which is well illustrated by the foreman-manager and couple of labourers living in a small isolated settlement. Whenever several months' supply of liquor was delivered, the foreman had to bury it.

A healthy rivalry, perhaps tinged with suspicion, exists between camp and Stanley, as well as between East and West Falkland. Some natural favouritism in the distribution of best mutton carcasses and sides of beef from camp to ex-campers and relatives in Stanley inevitably gives rise to some bad feeling, especially since the names of the recipients are announced over The Box.

To return to *Darwin*, our next stop was Fox Bay West. We seemed fated on this trip to arrive everywhere for breakfast. However, campers are always up early and are usually pleased to see fresh faces whatever the hour, Robin Robertson and her mother, both Australians, being no exception. From here we sailed on up the Sound to uninhabited Tyssen Island to collect sheep which had been left there to graze. We were met by the schooner *Ilen*, pronounced Eileen, one of many quaint island spellings like Burnt for Bernard. The men on the schooner worked the sheep on this particular group of islands, so this gave the *Darwin*'s crew an opporturtity to go ashore for an Upland Goose shoot. Scenically, the island was interesting with its huge clumps of tussac grass looking from the distance like miniature palm fronds, while on the far side of the Sound the high range of hills on West Falkland were still snow clad although it was well into summer. With the hundreds of Upland geese on the inland lake, grey tufted duck by the shore and penguins on the rocks it was a bird watcher's paradise.

It was interesting to watch the men working the sheep which had been penned in the shed by the shore and driven out of it onto the ship's gangway leading up onto the high prow of the scow. As they hesitated on the brink they were either forced to jump, or if recalcitrant, were hurled down. We joined a scow load of sheep on our way back to *Darwin*; clambering onto the scow by the same way, but were assisted down more gently. On our arrival at the side of the ship, however, we passengers had to climb and scramble whereas the sheep were hoisted aboard. Somewhere along the way we had off-loaded a horse, which had travelled in state hemmed in safely by the high sides of a gangway, where it was generally fussed over, unlike the countless sheep which now took its place, huddled together without fodder but once aboard silent and inert, reminding one of the saying, 'led like lambs to the slaughter'.

From here we sailed overnight to another uninhabited islet to collect more sheep. Bleaker Island is one of the many islands round the two main masses of East and West Falkland, many of which are uninhabited or have one family leading a lonely existence. We arrived so early it was not worth our while attempting to go ashore; we contented ourselves instead with watching activities through field glasses and a large sea elephant lazing on a shingle beach nearby. We sailed on up the east coast back to Stanley, past the two rocky islets thickly covered with tussac, past the silver sands and sand dunes of York Bay, past Pembroke lighthouse and through the Narrows on a cold sunny afternoon into Stanley harbour, feeling toned up from the fresh sea breezes to say nothing of muscles well exercised.

A camp trip is an interesting facet of island life, which I am glad to have experienced before RMS *Darwin*'s withdrawal from the local scene made it a thing of the past. It gave one a closer understanding of the idiosyncracies and contradictions of people thrown back on their own resources.

I found them independent yet lacking self-confidence; with a delightfully whimsical sense of humour yet inherently dour; earthy and bawdy yet convention-bound behind a set of semi-Victorian mores; unsophisticated and naïve yet nobody's fool; conservative and resistant to new ideas yet in their own way adaptable. Sea locked, and to some extent land-locked, into a rigid society and way of life, with little change over the years, the even tempo of camp life is broken only by the Beaver. People in camp have grown to accept the isolation and the way of life it imposes; a hard life where when grazing is poor, the cattle feed on kelp by the shore, and peat fibres are found in the sheep's kidneys.

The Kelper's are suspicious of the slow but inevitable advance of civilisation, and see it as a threat to their individuality. The fey quality of the islander which emerges when you get to know him, remains as enigmatic as the islands' stone runs, which have puzzled everyone from Darwin onwards. This geological feature, which is peculiar to the Falklands, consists of rivers of huge grey boulders covered with lichen under which lies a layer of small clean stones from where the water can be heard trickling. These stone runs wind down hillsides, according to the light, dull grey or gleaming like molten silver.

Chapter 15
Love to Mabel

Lack of communications within the islands had been a longstanding problem, when the only means was on horseback along the original routes laid out by the early settlers or by sea. Now that the Falklands government air service operates two de Havilland Beaver float planes, however, the colony has been for some time surprisingly well served internally. The air service has been active since 1948, the Governor, Sir Miles Clifford, being responsible for its introduction.

In an amusing account in the 1971 edition of the *Falkland Islands Journal* entitled 'The Birth of an Air Service', Sir Miles Clifford describes how the solution to the problem of isolation almost literally hit him. While travelling on the *Fitzroy* to visit Antarctic bases in 1947, he had taken a box of books and magazines for the FIDS. While the small ship bucked and reared its way south, the box fell from the bunk above, narrowly missing him. A copy of the *Reader's Digest* providentially landed by him and he soon found himself engrossed in an account of the flying doctor service.

Soon after this, for a few hundred pounds apiece, the Falkland Islands government bought two Auster aircraft, initially for land operations, but they were later put on floats because most settlements were located near water. Like the people of the outback of Australia, the Falkland Islanders soon became air minded and the air service has become akin to a daily taxi service. The aircraft carry five passengers, mail, medicines, freight, medical cases, the occasional corpse as well as miscellaneous livestock, though sheepdogs have not been welcomed as passengers since the hydatid disease scare. Flight schedules are made up daily and passenger lists and details of settlements to be visited are broadcast every evening over the local radio. The planes do not follow a regular route but pick up and put down passengers according to the bookings for that particular day.

Jim Kerr, director of civil aviation, Ian Campbell, the pilot, and Bert Conchie, the relief pilot who was on loan from the RAF while we were on the islands, do a first-class job, putting in long hours, flying in all weathers, much of it adverse. Weather in the islands can be so unpredictable that a day which starts off well may, despite Danny's forecast, deteriorate rapidly, entailing a return in gusting winds in the late afternoon or in the sudden sullen darkness of a winter's evening.

The planes were seldom held up for long, as the pilots are highly skilled and know every field, paddock, dyke, gate, rock, valley, mountain peak and air current blindfold, and even nervous passengers felt very safe in their capable hands. So expert and familiar with the terrain are the two pilots that despite the islands' freakish weather, there is seldom any significant backlog of passengers, except perhaps in the few days following one of the colony's major annual events, such as the Stanley sports meeting.

Jim Kerr, the more experienced pilot, is a canny Scot who had come to the islands after service in the RAF and had settled there with his wife, producing a Falkland Islands

15. Beaver float plane and launch taken from the *Darwin*.

family. Ian Campbell, an islander, took on a more daredevil approach to his flying; given to gate hopping and flying level with the telegraph wires as he zoomed past Sulivan House before making a dashing landing near the hangar.

Bert Conchie, the relief pilot, had much experience flying to bases down south; a natural loner, he loved the islands and the additional experience it gave him, some of the best and most interesting in the world. John always said it was real flying and regretted that time and work prevented him from joining them more often. He was able to accompany pilots on a fair number of occasions, introducing delegations and visiting VIPs to camp and taking part in mail drops.

These flights always took place after the arrival of *Darwin* or *AES*. Early the day after the mail had been sorted, when normally no passengers flew, the Beavers took off loaded with labelled mail bags most of which were dropped in flight with the pilot making a low approach at 50 feet to the paddock nearest the manager's house, there to push the bag out of the window. This is a relatively straightforward exercise when the approach and get-away are over comparatively flat ground, but a number of settlements are in small coastal clearings with mountains behind, and here, depending on the wind direction, the approach and get-away can be hazardous and particularly exciting for someone like John with a flying background, where the steep gliding approach and full engine climb, threading a path through the encircling hills, calls for a high degree of skill and judgement. Similarly the mail pickups would take place 48 hours before *Darwin*'s departure for Montevideo.

The hangar was not far from Sulivan House and I never tired of watching the Jumbo jets, as Stan called them, take off up or across the harbour, according to the wind direction, and occasionally chugging up to take off from our hulk, the *Jhelum*. I always watched out for their landing in the afternoon, the distinctive scarlet flash of the aircraft on its silver floats easily visible whatever the weather.

After a quarter of a century, the air service had become an integral part of island life, but in a world of spiralling inflation the cost of replacing the Beavers is formidable. During our time in the islands fares were comparatively cheap, roughly £5 a flight, but the hidden government subsidy ran at somewhere between £5000 and £10,000 a year.

The flexibility of this form of transport was demonstrated when decimilisation was introduced. Following talks over The

Box to familiarise islanders with the new currency, all old coins were collected from and new ones delivered to camp by Beaver – the changeover taking place within 48 hours. Incidentally, the 10/– note was retained in the islands as a 50p note.

As one could never rely on weather conditions, nor my reactions to them, and as travelling by Beaver could be extremely chilly, I had previously, out of consideration for both John and the pilot, not inflicted myself on them. However, I was determined to do one Beaver flip before leaving the colony and as a special privilege was allowed to take John's seat alongside the pilot, Jim Kerr.

Clad in the usual garb of anorak, trousers and boots, plus several layers of woollies, we turned up at the hangar at around 9.00 a.m. in uncertain misty weather. We hung about waiting for the mist to lift, but it was not long before Jim gave us the OK sign. The Beaver was pushed out of the hangar and at the head of the slipway we clambered onto the float and into an incredibly tiny cockpit, so far the only passengers. Having fastened our seatbelts we took off with a roar in a cloud of spray gaining height over Twelve O'Clock Mountain on the other side of the harbour.

We were just about to hop over the mountain when Jim did a tight turn and we zoomed back, landing once more near the hangar in response to a summons by one of the technicians who had been whirling a ground sheet round his head like a dervish. A late call had gone through to the hospital for medicine and Dr Ashmore was there with a package to be delivered to an outlying island.

We took off again, this time bumping in the upcurrents over the hill, flying low over penguin rookeries surprisingly far inland and all scuttling madly at the sound of the engine. We flew up Berkeley Sound landing at Port Louis in approximately 20 minutes to pick up two camp schoolchildren on their way to Darwin boarding school. A few minutes later we arrived at our destination, Salvador, to find Gene and Robin Pitaluga on the jetty seeing off a stiff upper-lipped small son to school. If weather and tide conditions are favourable when the Beaver lands at camp settlements, it motors gently alongside the jetty; otherwise, one has to clamber out into a small boat to be rowed ashore.

Our visit was to say goodbye to the Pitalugas and at the end of a pleasant afternoon Jim Kerr returned to collect us. As he buzzed the settlement we started to walk down to the jetty, where we found that Jim had already landed and was taking the opportunity to have smoko. This time the tide was low and Robin had to row us out in the dinghy to clamber aboard. We were again the only passengers and Jim thoughtfully went out of his way to pass over the flat tract of land where the legally protected wild cattle roam before flying over Volunteer Rocks to show us the fur seal colony clustered there. On the return leg I was able to take some aerial shots as we flew low over Stanley to the hangar, where I clambered out feeling lightheaded.

The two technicians, short-term volunteers from the RAF do a tour of duty of eighteen months to two years, and perform miracles of maintenance in all weathers. Clad in thigh-length waders they stride into the icy waters to meet the Beavers and guide them to the slipway. From there the plane is attached to a Land Rover to be hauled up and into the hangar, where it is thoroughly hosed down with fresh water each evening.

Internal communications were also kept open by RMS *Darwin* making coastal voyages to the settlements in between the once-monthly Montevidean schedules and also by MV *Forrest*, named after the Reverend Forrest, a former Tabernacle minister who was very popular with the island community. The *Forrest*, a government-owned small cargo vessel under the command of Jack Sollis with room for two hardy passengers, made regular trips round the islands delivering stores and performing a seaborne Pickfords service. She also performed the useful function of dumping rusting metal, old cars and such like eyesores at sea during the government-organised Operation Clean-Up.

The hovercraft, still at that time performing trial runs which sometimes turned into endurance tests, had been in service to the islands for several years. The islands terrain and waterways afford excellent hovercraft country and much useful expertise has been built up to be employed on the navy's new hovercraft, the BH7. It was a common sight to see the craft buzzing in and out of Stanley harbour in clouds of spray both day and night, when we were frequently wakened by its noisy departure. The Hovercraft Unit frequently visited settlements, on occasions taking mail and, in the context of its own operations, supplementing the communications service to settlements. From time to time it did a 'beef run' to replenish supplies at the Head of the Bay.

Adverse sea and weather conditions, particularly the heavy surf on the beaches, at times subjected the hovercraft to excessive hammerings. On one unfortunate occasion when it took off on a cold wintry afternoon and, off Billy Rocks, the weather deteriorated rapidly. A freak sea stove in the forward hatch and it was only the skill of the pilot which brought it ashore on the beach opposite Kidney Island. Contact was lost and the worst feared. A search party comprised of Marines, Ted Clapp of BAS and members of the FIDF set out. Flares were eventually spotted and it was a relief to know that the hovercraft and its crew had reached shore in safety. The craft was by then nearing the end of its useful life and when we left it seemed probable that MV *Forrest* would be taking over its role as a vehicle for the Marines.

The government-operated radio telephone service plays an essential part in islands communications keeping the forty-odd settlements in touch with Stanley and each other. The colony has Sir Miles Clifford to thank for that particular godsend to the busy housewife as she tunes in while at her Rayburn each morning to listen to the daily weather reports from camp settlements as well as the day's gossip. The network also fulfils the role of a flying doctor service with medical officers in Stanley able to give advice to patients in camp and when accidents are reported, a Beaver can, if necessary, be alerted at short notice. Edith McMullen, or Radio Edith as she is codenamed and popularly known everywhere in the islands, received a well-deserved decoration recently in the New Year's honours list. At the controls daily, morning and afternoon, she tunes in to the settlements. The radio telephone however is public, consequently all gossip is common knowledge down to the most intimate detail.

The wireless station a few miles out of Stanley, and Cable & Wireless, link the islands with the world outside, while the European Space Research Organisation and BAS have teleprinter links with their headquarters in Europe and Britain. The overseas telegraph and telephone link was with London. There was no direct service with South America and traffic for that continent had to he routed through London. An Argentine ship-to-shore station, the General Pacheco, maintained a daily 20-second morning schedule at about 9.30 with the Stanley ship-to-shore radio and, in case of urgency messages could be passed on this channel. As we shall see, this channel was later developed as the link between Argentina and the colony when telecommunications were freed after the second round of talks in Buenos Aires in mid-1971.

The local radio, known by everybody as 'The Box', and almost a personality in its own right, is a rediffusion system connected from the government studio to loudspeakers in practically every house in Stanley and was run by Charlie Rieve. The yearly rental is minimal. It is kept turned up day and night for public announcements, which are always preceded by the same piece of martial music played for several minutes, to allow the housewife time to drop what she is doing in order to make a mad dash to the kitchen, its usual abode, to hear exciting events such as that 17 bags of mail have arrived by *Darwin*, or that parcel mail from *AES* is now ready for collection at the gymnasium, or a long list of sweets and chocolates available in one of the smaller stores, or that fish is on sale at the corner of John Street, or a cinema announcement.

Every morning, except Sundays, broadcasting begins at 8.00 a.m. in summer, 9.00 a.m. in winter, with relayed BBC news to be followed by weather and morning music for the housewife, which is often a listener's choice type programme. Transmission ends at midday, usually with a local announcement or a for sale notice, to begin again in the evening at 6.30 p.m. in winter, 7.30 p.m. in summer, except Saturdays when transmission begins earlier with a programme for children. On Sunday evenings listening is more limited, the highlight being a half-hour broadcast 'Calling the Falklands', a programme of record requests and messages from relatives and friends in Britain, relayed by the BBC.

When not long before we left, a BBC engineer came out to the islands to survey and make recommendations on updating the radio service, a plea was put to him to improve the quality of reception of this vital programme. Religious programmes rate next, with the three denominations taking it in turns to broadcast their services but the Anglican has the edge over the other two as the Governor traditionally attends the Anglican cathedral, where it is customary for him to read the lesson. Whenever he attends church the national anthem is played at the conclusion of the service. Evening broadcasts begin with weather forecast and flight schedules followed by messages and announcements. A typical message runs as follows: 'Good flight – arrived 4.00 p.m. Thanks for lovely holiday, Love X,' relayed by some camper who had arrived in Stanley by Beaver a few hours earlier. A local announcement could be as follows: 'For Sale – Baby Bouncer' (there was obviously a plethora of this item in the islands) or, 'Wanted – 2 navvies and 1 roustabout for San Carlos', and frequently, 'Wanted urgently – a maid for Darwin Boarding School', with details of hours and salary. Anything for sale is quickly swallowed up in the islands due to the scarcity of goods. When we were packing up a list of our household goods was relayed and the telephone was red hot before the announcement was over.

BBC news and radio newsreel can be heard from the studio and old favourites such as Tony Hancock's Half Hour, the Goon show and vintage programmes of the Archers are particularly popular, with the omnibus edition of the latter being put out on Saturday mornings. In the islands, the episodes of the Archers are several years behind those being broadcast in England and one islander on her way to Britain on the *AES*, found herself all at sea when she avidly tuned in for the latest developments!

Local programmes of talks, quizzes and record requests are relayed, the latter being the most popular. Records are sent in by locals for locals and patients in hospital and some favourites make their appearance time and time again. Children's record request programme, Little Sir Echo, follows the same routine on Saturday afternoon when birthday records are regular features along with messages to the child concerned to find his or her present hidden in a hidey hole such as the washing machine. It often seemed to me as if Falkland Islands children had several birthdays a year.

One of the most popular weekly programmes is the Friday night newsletter to which everyone listens, including I am told people in Patagonia, to be brought up to date with shipping details, passenger details, government business, births, deaths, marriages, whist drives and other local news, as well as material from overseas newspapers and correspondence. As there is no daily newspaper in the islands the newsletter fills the gap to a certain extent.

A small panel of two or three newsreaders, working on a weekly rotation, collects and presents the material for the Friday newsletter. Ted Clapp of the BAS is a popular newsreader, while Bert Conchie, the relief pilot, was expert at providing topical news from his daily contacts with camp. Another popular feature is visitors' corner, which, as its name implies, consists of interviews with distinguished and interesting visitors to the colony. In our day, A. G. Barton (AGB) ably performed the interviewing for this programme. On occasions, visitors with specialised interests would be asked to give a talk; General Lathbury gave an interesting talk on birds and Sir Vivien Fuchs a fascinating account of Antarctic travel hazards.

Commentaries on sheepdog trials, race meetings, the May Ball and similar functions are also broadcast. Sidney Miller's annual commentary on the sheepdog trials being a firm favourite with the island public on account of his graphic language, while René Rowlands or Joyce Kerr expertly commented on dresses and cakes.

Falkland Islands reunions taped in Britain also make good listening. These take place annually in London and always succeed in sounding like an orgy. Against a noisy background the islanders are invited to speak into the microphone to relay messages about the fine time they are having, always finishing by sending love to a lengthy list of brothers, aunts and cousins among whom Mabel always seemed to appear! 'Love to Mabel' became one of our Sulivan House catch phrases. At 10.00 or 11.00, according to the season, the national anthem is played at the conclusion to the day's broadcasting.

The daily broadcasts contain the legacies of several Governors. One Governor, an avid cricket fan, arranged for test matches to be broadcast before the morning news and at lunch time. Although there is a flourishing cricket club in Stanley, I expect this is one time when The Box is turned off in most Falkland Islands households. The latest legacy is the stock exchange report at the end of the day's programme.

The only published news media in the islands are the *Monthly Review* and religious news sheets giving minutiae of island life. There is nothing else except the *Fakland Islands Journal*, an annual publication containing material from archives, specially commissioned articles and historical reminiscences. John and I enjoyed editing this publication during our time there.

In marked contrast with the good internal communications, the external communications were marginal, consisting of the once monthly sailing to and from Montevideo, the arrival of the cargo-cult ship three or four times a year and the ephemeral unscheduled movements of naval and BAS ships. The winter seemed even longer by *Darwin's* removal for annual maintenance in Montevideo and the islands were completely cut off from the outside world.

People going on leave with connections to catch in Monte often spent the voyage mentally pushing the boat on, for if *Darwin* were delayed by rough seas and head winds, onward bookings were reserved for a limited time only. By the same token, if someone coming in the opposite direction cut aeroplane schedules too finely, missing a connection, *Darwin* might sail without him, entailing a stopover in Uruguay for at least a month. Another worry one learned to live with was that in the event of an emergency, such as bad news from Britain, if there were no *Darwin* or *AES* in harbour, there was absolutely nothing one could do about it. From time to time, Marines had to leave hurriedly in response to a family SOS and the Falkland Islands government would do everything to facilitate their departure. I remember one occasion which entailed flying a Marine out by Beaver to a New Zealand cargo ship, which fortuitously was passing up the Falkland Sound. The Marine was in luck as, although the army normally does everything in its power to fly soldiers home in such cases, it would have been impossible for them to send transport to so remote a spot.

All in all, with constant practice and repetition in a tight domestic environment, internal communications ran smoothly and efficiently. The recurrent costs of the services was soaring in line with escalating costs elsewhere in the world, necessitating the Falkland Islands government to increase its uneconomic subsidies, while the equipment – the Beavers and radio transmitting gear – was nearing the end of its useful life.

Replacements at 1970s costs would put too much strain on the colony's capital resources and an appeal would probably have to be made for British aid. MV *Forrest*, being less than five years old, was the only modern ship, but her role had been designed to serve the old system of internal communications. She might not be suitable for a different role in a new communications pattern. A similar problem faced external communications. It would be uneconomic to replace the ageing *Darwin*, which was already swallowing up too much of the company's and the taxpayers' money. In such circumstances, it was imperative to find a practicable as well as a viable alternative.

Chapter 16
End of an Era

Once more the Antarctic season was drawing to a close. One by one the ships sailed northwards and winter, never far away at any time, was upon us with a vengeance, with biting winds and flurries of snow and hail sweeping across the harbour. The Queen's Birthday parade was held in even filthier weather than usual, followed by the annual Government House ball on a real winter's night. *Bransfield*, the last of the northbound ships was still in port, enabling Captain Woodfield and his officers to attend, which made a pleasant change for the ladies and a relief for many of the husbands who could now slope off to the billiard room with an easy conscience.

One face missing from the party was that of first officer John Morton, who had an unfortunate fall on board ship while down south and had left on *Darwin*, his foot in plaster, to find later in hospital in Britain that it had been badly set. His highly promising career with BAS looked as if it might have come to an end. Chris Elliot, the young second officer, took over and ably shouldered the unexpected responsibility thrust upon him.

Instead of the colony closing down and retreating into its customary period of isolation, the build up to the second round of talks, to be held in Buenos Aires, began and a trickle of visitors for this purpose was already beginning to penetrate the southern mid-winter barrier; once underway, events moved with startling rapidity.

Accompanying John Morton on the same northbound sailing of *Darwin* were the two members of staff of Peat, Marwick & Mitchell, the international consultants commissioned under British aid to make recommendations for a viable future internal and external transport pattern for the colony. We saw them off, both of them apprehensively taking 'Dutch courage' to bolster their already fluttering stomachs. The ship was filled to capacity and they were placed in the hospital for the rough journey ahead.

The two young men, one a Scot, the other a New Zealand Rhodes scholar, had arrived by the previous *Darwin*'s crossing, hence their apprehension, to spend an arduous month investigating, assessing and reporting on this vital issue. Lights burned late in the Secretariat as they worked flat out gathering and analysing material for their report. In addition, they visited the camp, inspected possible sites for an airfield, met most of the inhabitants and asked searching questions of everyone they met. In addition, they managed to fit a few social engagements into a tight schedule. I had to laugh at the Scot's traumatic shock, similar to my own, at prevailing conditions, whereas the New Zealander accepted them without question.

Whenever we had a moment to spare John and I would begin to make plans for our leave. Before the landslide became an avalanche, much planning, diplomatic activity and paperwork had to be completed. Isolated as we were, it was necessary to begin plotting our journey to Europe at least nine months beforehand, as it often took six months or more to get answers to queries put to shipping companies and hotels. In fact, some did not even bother to reply, while one reply from a hotel in Chile reached us three months after we had arrived back in Europe. This was the other side of the coin encountered during our first year in the islands when we received dunning letters threatening legal action for goods which had not even arrived and which were probably sitting in some London dock awaiting the sailing of *AES*.

After consuming the *South American Handbook*, which became my Bible until it was proved wrong on several occasions, Paraguay became our Mecca, with a riverboat as our chosen mode of transport from Buenos Aires. The reason for our choice was that Paraguay was the direct antithesis to life in the islands, and its climate, conditions and people reminded us of West Africa. In addition, its history and people intrigued us. Here was a country with a national identity forged in the stress of war, a distinct contrast to the lack of it from which Uruguay and Argentina appeared to us to suffer. Despite various setbacks we were later to sail through the jungle country of the Chaco to Asunción, with Graham Greene's book *Travel with My Aunt* fittingly at my elbow.

Not least of our setbacks was our 'non-arrival' in Argentina. The policy makers had slipped up. Since the signing of the joint statement people travelling from the islands had gone straight on to the UK by air or sea and the immigration officials involved were *au fait* with the situation. We found to our cost, however, that travel agents and other such bodies had never heard of said declaration, let alone the travel cards issued to all island residents for passing through Argentina. There was nothing for it but to set out, hot foot and irate, for the British embassy.

By June the groundwork had been laid for the second round of talks, to be preceded by a visit to the colony of the British members of our delegation. At this point, to present a coherent picture of the background to the communications problem in general and to demonstrate in particular the interaction of the

Falkland Island Company and the Falkland Islands' government which is set far back in the colony's history, I shall endeavour to pull together the strands of the tangled skein and so lead up to the final solution.

Until the Panama Canal was opened, the Falkland Islands, because of its geographical location some 400 miles west-northwest of the Horn, benefited from the ship repair business. Many a sailing ship limped into the haven of Stanley harbour after a perilous passage. Incidentally, one of those was our hulk, the *Jhelum*, an East Indiaman said to be the best surviving example of its type of vessel in the world. After the usual difficult passage rounding the Horn, her last voyage ended in Stanley in August 1870. The crew had refused to put to sea again and as a result she was surveyed and condemned, to end her days opposite Sulivan House.

With the opening of the Panama Canal in 1855 the ship repair business dwindled, while after the battles of Coronel and the Falkland Islands during the First World War, the colony lost its strategic position as a naval standby base. A naval presence continued and continues to this day, but on a much reduced scale. The colony at that time had been well served with shipping communications, with ocean-going liners calling every two weeks, which compared favourably with what existed fifty years later.

After the First World War the colony's communications were principally maintained by ships of the Falkland Islands Company. These ships, regularly sailing the 1000-mile journey from Montevideo to Stanley, were then a paying proposition. In a settled, pre-1939 world, they were able to carry the colony's passenger traffic as well as its wool exports.

Coincidental with the postwar recession in the shipping business, during his nine-year period in office President Peron of Argentina revived, in explit form, his country's claim to sovereignty over the Falkland Islands, which no doubt served as a distraction from his country's internal problems.

It is not necessary here to go in depth into the sovereignty argument. In brief, after the war of liberation in South America at the turn of the eighteenth-century, the Republic of Argentina claimed sovereignty over the Falkland Islands in succession to the Spanish settlement which had been there. The Argentine settlement of Puerto Soledad was destroyed following a sealing dispute with America and was abandoned. This action by the Americans arose because of their impatience at the lack of control of sealing operations around the islands.

The British, who had previously established a settlement in the colony, returned to the islands, reoccupying them unopposed, to build up the sheep industry, which is now the colony's main economic base. The Falkland Islands Company gradually became prominent and, with more than 50 per cent of the land, is today the largest landowner in the colony.

Peron's actions were aimed at isolating the colony, which turned its orientation even more towards Europe than had previously been the case. In the Second World War many volunteers of British extraction from Argentina had served on a voluntary basis in the armed services of Britain in the colony. Many families in the Falkland Islands were and still are closely related to farmers in the part of Patagonia which lies opposite the colony, particularly in the area near Rio Gallegos. These links became tenuous, although they were not broken. In particular, links were maintained through the enthusiastic use of amateur radio by a number of inhabitants. Although Peron was partially successful in cutting the colony off from the Argentine mainland, complete contact was not lost. Peron's aim was to create misunderstanding between the two communities and in this he succeeded. The island community and the people of Argentina became increasingly ignorant at first hand of developments in each other's land areas.

A result of the Peron policy of isolating the colony was to strengthen the latter's links with Uruguay. When the Falkland Islands Company's ship RMS *Darwin,* taking over from the *Fitzroy*, started to ply the route between the colony's capital of Stanley and Montevideo in 1958 the colony's external communications consisted primarily of this single ship, which sailed 12 times a year. Built as a passenger and cargo ship, the *Darwin* never fulfilled its cargo-carrying role externally. Consequently, as economics relentlessly overtook the passenger shipping trade, *Darwin* became a drain on the resources of the Falkland Islands Company and the possibility that she would not be replaced as her working life drew to a close was recognised though not easily accepted. By the mid-1960s the company was increasingly doubtful about the economic wisdom of replacing their ship. As handling charges in Montevideo had become exorbitant and were becoming more so with spiralling inflation in Uruguay, *Darwin*'s holds were practically empty. To give an example, sheep imported from New Zealand to improve Falkland Island stocks cost as much to transport from New Zealand to Carrasco by air freight as from the airport to Montevidean docks.

It was in the light of this situation that, late in 1968, the Falkland Islands government sought the aid of the British government to carry out a survey into the feasibility of constructing an airfield in the colony suitable for the operation of an external air service. As readers already know, the colony was air-minded and so the projected survey was not as radical a departure as might seem on the face of it. However, there were grave doubts about whether the terrain, primarily covered with peat and, according to the season, alternately dry and brittle or soggily wet, would be found capable of providing a sufficiently firm base to support an airfield.

The area tentatively selected for the survey lay near Cape Pembroke, five miles east-northeast of Stanley. Board of Trade officials carried out the feasibility survey. After examining alternatives to the Cape Pembroke site the survey report recommended that an airfield at Cape Pembroke was feasible. Costs early in 1969 for an airfield with two runways were estimated, with associated equipment, in particular navigational equipment, at some £325,000. I understand that the figure has now soared to nearly £2 million.

Funds of this order were not available from the colony's own resources; nor was it politically certain that an airlield was an acceptable solution to the colony's problems. The recrudescence of the Argentinian claim to sovereignty over the colony in 1968 exacerbated the situation. Meanwhile, RMS *Darwin* was entering the last five years of her useful life.

Faced with this situation, the Executive Council's first job was to appoint a fact-finding survey of the colony's transport communications. It then appointed a subcommittee to examine possible solutions for future patterns of transport communications and to make recommendations. The Colonial Secretary chaired the subcommittee, and the Colonial Manager of the Falkland Islands Company and the colony's representative of Cable & Wireless Ltd served as the other two members. All three were expatriates.

Appointed at the end of 1969, the subcommittee reported early in 1970 to the Executive Council, recommending that the colony's main external passenger transport link should be airborne. In principle, the Executive Council accepted this recommendation shortly before the first round of talks on the colony's communications between Britain and Argentina.

The 1970 talks were exploratory and in the course of them the Argentine side made a number of offers designed to free communications between the colony and the Argentine mainland, among which was one to construct an airfield in the colony and to operate an air service to it.

The talks were confidential. Unused as they were to the niceties and tortuousness of international negotiation, the inhabitants of the Falkland Islands naturally suspected that secret agreements might have been arrived at in London. An uneasy period followed, exacerbated by an announcement by the Falkland Islands Company that RMS *Darwin* would be withdrawn from service at the end of 1971, thus severing the colony's passenger link with the South American mainland. However, the eventual publication in the colony of the content of the 1970 talks cleared the air and the islanders were taken into the government's confidence. As a facet of this exercise, the British government agreed to finance from aid funds a study of the colony's transport system as a follow up to the Executive Council's amateur study of the same subject.

The international consultants, Peat, Marwick & Mitchell, were appointed to carry out this task, which they performed with commendable speed in the space of three months. A well-researched report was the result of a visit to the colony by two members and to the Argentine mainland by one other member of the consultants' staff. Their report in broad outline confirmed the Executive Council's proposals, though it presented them in greater depth and detail and examined alternative communications vehicles and methods. Basically, the report suggested that an external transport system consisting of aircraft as the main passenger-carrying vehicle, combined with a single ship capable of fulfilling the round the islands role but with the capability of making voyages to the mainland, would be the most economical solution.

The second round of talks on communications between Britain and Argentina took place soon afterwards in Buenos Aires, in June and July 1971. The colony was again represented by three members of its Legislative Council, with the Colonial Secretary again heading the islands representation. Because the Falkland Islands Company owned 50 per cent of the colony's land and produced so large a proportion of the wool crop, it seemed logical to island opinion and in the company's own interest that they would probably provide the shipping links.

Before the Buenos Aires talks took place, the British members of the delegation, led by David Scott of the Foreign and Commonwealth Office, were picked up on the mainland by the *AES* and brought to Stanley to spend a week in the colony, holding a series of meetings with the Executive and Legislative Councils, and making numerous visits to the settlements to give the campers a chance to ask questions and air their views. It also enabled the British team to experience the rugged conditions and communications difficulties that had hitherto only existed for them in files.

For the first time a government reception was held in the Town Hall in Stanley with the Colonial Secretary and his wife as hosts, to enable the three-man team to 'meet the people'. About two hundred and fifty attended. The Upland Goose, the most southerly British hotel in the world, carried out the catering and beverages were restricted to soft drinks, beer or sherry to reduce costs and keep down exuberance. On other occasions the team was treated to the customary lavish island hospitality, as well the usual round of cocktail and dinner parties at Government House.

An 'Any Questions' programme was broadcast, islanders having been invited to send in questions to the delegation, which were answered live in an impromptu session in Government House with Ted Clapp of BAS as question master. The Foreign and Commonwealth Office, the Falkland Islands government and the Falkland Islands Company were all represented. This gave the British members of the team a no-holds-barred exposure and further enabled them to assess island opinion. The islanders, if not exactly disarmed, became more relaxed as a result of the exercise.

The atmosphere was already more relaxed after the revelation of the harmless nature of the 1970 talks. It was increasingly apparent that opinion was becoming not only reconciled to, but in favour of, the idea of some kind of external air link. Parents of children being educated in Montevideo were apprehensive about a future without *Darwin*, while the colony as a whole was naturally worried about urgent medical cases, not to mention mail. The sincerity of the without strings offer made in the 1970 talks to send in an Argentine Air Force amphibian aircraft should the need arise for urgent medical attention had been put to the test and had a steadying effect on public opinion in the colony.

The mercy flight had brought home to the islanders the urgency of the need for some form of rapid external communication with South America. A further reminder that some solution with Argentina must be sought arose when the BAS had to transport two members of the Secretariat staff to Punta Arenas and from there send them by plane via Santiago to the British hospital in Montevideo. The *Darwin* was between sailing schedules, the *AES* on the high seas and it was medically advisable for both to reach hospital as soon as possible. Fortunately, a BAS ship in port was about to sail for Punta Arenas and so was able to come to the rescue.

Despite such reminders, the hardliners were still unwilling to be won over and were ready to read into any change a threat to their sovereignty. Many islanders were at that time still sceptical of the outcome of the second round of talks, preferring instead to reserve judgement until something concrete materialised and, as usual, rumour was rife in Stanley. Before the British and Falkland Islands delegations left the colony, David Scott made a broadcast to reassure the people of the British government's intentions. As the islanders were by now hardened to blandly delivered platitudes and were inclined to look for the pill under the sugar coating, the talk was received with some cynicism. It was unfortunate that at the same time Maurice Waldron, chairman of the Falkland Islands Company, who was visiting the colony, broadcast a message of reassurance about the company's future intentions in the field of transport. The unedifying spectacle, doubtless unwitting, was of Scott and Wadron competing in the business of making soothing noises.

In the midst of the frenetic round of receptions, dinners and cocktail parties, inseperable from such visits, John and I went down with one of those virulent flu bugs imported from the outside world. We were paying the price of our isolation and fast losing our immunity to such germs, to the extent that, as with the rest of Stanley, a common cold that outsiders take in their stride turned into a major illness. John, well doped by Dr Ashmore, recovered sufficiently to leave with the delegation on the *AES*, which the British government had chartered to take them to Puerto Descado, while I succumbed to my flu in the solitude of Sulivan House. I was glad in a way to lie low as I was becoming tired of the effort of putting on and off the two faces of a Colonial Secretary's wife. Until 1969 life for previous Mrs Colonial Secretary had been tranquil and she had been able to sit back and ring those bells. Pinpricks aside, the team left feeling that it had the confidence of the majority of the islanders, but it became obvious to me that no sooner had they departed than island opinion, fickle at the best of times, gave way to pressure and did a volte-face.

No South American journey worth its salt is complete without its fiasco; once in port, there followed a Fred Karno act involving ladders, mud, car and planes and they eventually made it to Buenos Aires where a marathon round of meetings was held with the Argentinian team. The sessions, often lasting into the early hours of the morning, involved hard bargaining, endless drafting and several cliff-hanging moments before the compromise was reached, embodied in the joint statement of Buenos Aires of 1 July 1971, coinciding with my birthday, which I seemed fated to spend alone in the islands.

As the leader of the British delegation later said in a broadcast to the people of the colony, the Buenos Aires round of talks was tough, but it was also realistic and the representatives of the colony made a positive contribution to its outcome. The joint statement laid the basis of a revolution in the colony's transport communications system. The central conception was for an external air transport system to be Argentine operated, through a British-built airfield at Cape Pembroke near Stanley, and with the possibility of charter operators making non-scheduled flights, while a shipping service would be British operated. The agreement also covered a number of important aspects of communications such as travel documentation, telecommunications and mail, the defacement of which had long been an irritant in the colony. In the interim, until the British-built airfield in the colony was operational, the Argentine government undertook to provide a twice-monthly service with amphibious Albatross aircraft of its Air Force.

The Fakland Islands members of the delegation left Buenos Aires with the feeling of a job well done. To evaluate the merits of Comodoro Rivadavia and Rio Gallegos as a stopping point for the future air service, they returned via the latter, from where they were flown to Stanley in an amphibian of the Argentine Air Force. This was the second Albatross to land in Stanley harbour but this time on a cold frosty morning in reasonably calm conditions. The sun was just beginning to make its presence felt on the light sprinkling of snow, when the lumbering plane appeared, to circle overhead before coming down to land smoothly near the air service offices on the government jetty.

Meanwhile, the *Philomel* was still smouldering in Fairy Cove. Ted Clapp and his fire fighting crew had been up most of the night in sub zero temperatures combatting the fire on the blazing ship and now had a full day's work ahead of them.

A small welcoming party, with members of the Executive and Legislative Councils, was arranged in Government House for the returning members of the delegation, the Argentine Air Commodore in charge of the operational sector and Carlos Louge of the Malvinas department of the Argentine foreign ministry, who had accompanied them while some of the crew had soup and sandwiches in Sulivan House before setting out on a shopping foray. Speeches were made in a general spirit of euphoria and gifts exchanged.

This atmosphere persisted until the Albatross had taken off, whereupon the islanders' latent suspicious came to the fore. David Scott had taped a message to the colony in the Embassy in Buenos Aires, which was relayed on The Box. However, despite this, the hard work in Buenos Aires was followed by even harder work on the part of the Governor and Colonial Secretary to convince the islanders that the Joint Statement was not a sellout but, with goodwill on both sides, offered a basis for a better relationship for the future.

Looking at it objectively, I reckoned that the islanders had done well out of the bargaining as the Argentinians were generous to a fault, particularly in offers of scholarships and other educational opportunities, but I could also understand why many islanders took a different view, regarding the educational offers as Greek gifts. Within a few weeks Carlos

Louge was to return in the third Albatross to visit the islands. People were already becoming blasé about the amphibians; the Land Rover queues were only a few yards long and even the government horses did not bother to look up this time. Carlos Louge was accompanied by Colonel Balcarce, also of the Ministry of Foreign Affairs, and a three-man mission from the Argentine Air Force led by Vice-Commodore Degan Loeb with Major Carlos Bloomer-Reeve and the engineering expert, Major Remorino, as nice a bunch of servicemen you could hope to meet anywhere.

They were to undertake an investigation into the feasibility of constructing a temporary airfield capable of taking the Fokker F27 turbo-prop aircraft. They stayed at the Upland Goose hotel where, in the brief periods when they could take a rest they could be seen prodding the peat fire in an uncertain manner. At the same time, staying at Government House, were Colonel Wheatley of the Royal Engineers and Group Captain Freddy Melrose, Air Attaché to the British Embassy in Buenos Aires. Bob Wheatley carried out a further survey of the Cape Pembroke site with a view to evaluating whether the construction of the airfield could be advantageously effected by army construction units.

The weather was fine though frosty throughout this period. The wind did not blow, the sun shone and I sunbathed by an open window in the conservatory. A few flurries of snow fell, but the calm continued and the visiting team began to consider the notorious islands weather a myth, but the capricious Falklands winds, however, did not let us down. The day they were due to leave they were treated to a first-class gale which whipped the inner harbour into a frenzy. Takeoff was postponed several times and finally put off until next moring, the Upland Goose valiantly coping with extra beds and food for the air crew. Next morning they just managed to get off before winds again reached gale force and the weather deteriorated still further, putting a stop to the Beavers flying for several days.

Within a very short time of the signing of the joint statement it had become clear to the participants in the talks that construction of the Cape Pembroke airfield would be a lengthy operation with Stanley at the end of an 8000-mile pipeline. The Argentine Air Force had three Albatross amphibian aircraft and the Argentine Navy another three, but the fortnightly service to the Falkland Islands would necessitate the diversion from these duties of two aircraft, one for the task and the other for the backup, for a period of up to four or five days depending on the weather, which was notoriously changeable, between Comodoro Rivadavia, the departure point of the service from the Argentine mainland, and Stanley. Consequently, the Argentine government put forward a proposal to build a temporary airfield as a stopgap to relieve pressure on their Albatross amphibians.

It can readily be appreciated that such a proposal from the Argentine side, following almost immediately on the heels of the Buenos Aires agreement, roused misgivings among the islanders and reactivated their suspicions of Argentine motives. The islanders had become reconciled to the forthcoming external air service but, as is only human in such situations, they were now inclined to suspect the Latin Americans of carrying gifts of airfields. However, a combination of patience on the part of the Colony Government, allied to the stipulation of certain safeguards, carried the day and agreement for the temporary airfield project was given, and not only to the project but also to its being Argentine executed.

A Commonwealth parliamentary association delegation from the House of Commons, consisting of Mr Bernard Conlan, Labour, and Mr Richard Luce, Conservative, visited the colony at this time. They arrived by *Darwin* in time for the Remembrance Sunday Parade when, for once, the weather was kind and Stanley was at its best with the sun shining on a calm blue harbour and the gorse in full bloom, a blaze of yellow glory. The two parliamentarians had a blunt, down-to-earth approach, which hit the right note in the islands. They had meetings with the Executive and Legislative Councils, visited camp, and a second successful government reception was held in the Town Hall to enable them to meet the people.

Again the Colonial Secretary and his wife acted as hosts introducing the about 250 guests to the two MPs. They thus had the opportunity to satisfy themselves that the bulk of the islanders supported both the agreements reached in Buenos Aires and the subsequent proposals with regard to the temporary airfield, which would enable a far better service to be provided than was possible with the marginal operations of the amphibian.

Apart from the limitations the service to the islands would impose on their civilian role, these aircraft were subject to severe load-carrying limitations, their effective passenger carrying capacity being six, two of which would have to be retained until the last minute in the event of an emergency hospital case, while the uncertain weather conditions in the Stanley harbour area necessitated the use of expensive JATO Rockets in an assisted takeoff.

The two MPs had an opportunity to try out the Albatross service, to which Mr Conlan in particular had been looking forward, instead of the return *Darwin* trip. Once more they were treated to gale force winds, which delayed departure until late the following morning. Takeoffs were always anxious moments and it was a nerve-wracking experience to watch the Albatross (looking monstrous compared with the miniscule Beaver) roar into life, manoeuvre into position and take off striving for sufficient power in a cloud of spray before the blast off by rockets, their smoke leaving a vapour trail behind them as the plane climbed slowly over the surrounding hills.

These were still unscheduled flights bringing or lifting out VIPs and personnel connected with the forthcoming service to begin in January 1972. It was the end of an era. For my part I had found it intensely interesting to have a seat in the front row of the stalls. After the excitement of such live grand opera, it was almost an anticlimax to discover from observation and with some wry amusement that our visiting Argentine diplomats behaved more like stolid British whereas their Foreign and Commonwealth Office counterparts behaved more like volatile South Americans.

Chapter 17
Albatross Dawn

Late spring brought the onset of better weather and by Albatross the team sent by a firm of airfield consulting engineers to carry out the detailed work upon which invitations to tender for the airfield construction project would be based. The same men had previously built Lungyi airport in Freetown, so the arduous conditions at the Cape Pembroke site did not present any problem. They worked in the field as long as it was daylight and then at their drawing board calculations when it grew dark, winning the admiration of everyone in Stanley with their beaver-like way, bulldozing, digging holes and taking samples. In this they were unremittingly backed up by Superintendent of public works, Tom Royans, members of his department as well as specially recruited casual labour, who used to fascinate the team by producing hardboiled penguin eggs for smoko.

The site at Cape Pembroke soon became so full of large holes that that it had to be avoided by islanders accustomed to riding there at this time of year, their horses once more in from camp on their mowing machine exercise in Stanley gardens. We had this team of tough guys along to Sulivan House one Sunday for drinks before they became too involved in the job, working daily including the day of rest, after which one only caught occasional glimpses of them burned the colour of mahogany by the combination of sun and strong winds. They left the colony laden with sacks of soil and rock samples. The Albatross crew threw up their hands in horror and insisted on a meticulous weigh in. As always, weight limitations were critical for Albatross operations.

On account of so much activity winter seemed much shorter this year and the ships were back in November almost before Stanley had fully recovered from the last visit. The Season was soon in full swing with the usual feverish round of parties on board *Biscoe*, *Bransfield* and *Endurance*, as well as dinners and cocktail parties ashore in Stanley homes and at Government House where more than one islands resident was eased gently out, glassy eyed.

The British research ship *Shackleton*, formerly a BAS ship, paid a brief visit to Stanley, to the delight of some older residents whose sons were members of the crew. This season we were also visited by two ships of the Russian navy at a time when both *Bransfield* and *Endurance* were in port; at that particular cocktail party at Government House the gold braid was eye dazzling and the evening became almost hysterical with misunderstanding! December was a busy month with election fever on top of everything else.

The camp took a long time to dry out that year and it was not until Christmas day that John and I were able to have a really good walk to the River Murrel, about three miles out of Stanley, which does not sound far as the crow flies, but when one takes into account the steep hills, tussacy uneven ground, dodging patches of bog on the way and an omnipresent wind, the distance becomes twice as long. Once at the banks of the river we enjoyed the unexpected strip of sandy beach.

On the walk we had been surprised to see one of *Endurance*'s helicopters quartering the ground ahead and had assumed that a fishing party had been organised. We had just arrived back at Moody Brook and were about to drive off when a member of the Hovercraft Unit came dashing out to inform John that a R/T report had come in from a camp settlement that a riderless horse had returned there. Several search parties had already set out, including the helicopter; the Hovercraft Unit and Marines had been alerted to follow suit, which put paid to their Christmas day off. We stayed till the hovercraft left the hangar and went speeding out towards the Narrows. The party of Marines soon found the 'camper' in question, who had set out for Stanley after 'celebrating the peace', as Stan described it, where he lay stoned on the banks of the River Murrel, not far from where we had been earlier. That crisis over we were able to enjoy a pleasant Christmas dinner party at Government House.

Over the Christmas period race meetings were held in fitful sunshine with mid-summer snow squalls thrown in for good measure, but they were as usual well attended by Stanley residents, campers and naval and BAS personnel who were spending the festive season in port. At the New Year ball local husbands were again in luck as *Bransfield* was still tied up at the Public jetty. It was an enjoyable evening with the Governor in fine fettle dashing along the corridor outside the ballroom, to reappear nonchalantly, glass in hand, at the other entrance, occasioning one guest at the door to remark, 'I wish HE would go round the other way. He's making me dizzy.'

I had already started to pack in December, to everyone's surprise, but long experience in West Africa had taught me to have all trunks and boxes crated and banded well in advance of departure. In this do-it-yourself country with no steward boy to assist and where I even wielded a paint brush to write 'Stanley to Soton via BAS' with other detailed particulars, it was necessary to begin even earlier. At that time round three was still scheduled to take place in late February or early March so it was even more essential to have everything ready well beforehand as we would be leaving immediately afterwards.

In between selling possessions via The Box and organising the 1972 edition of *The Falkland Islands Journal* I packed steadily until our drawing room was taken over by boxes and trunks. Everything was nailed down by the end of January, thus giving me time to concentrate on the final editing of the journal. The Governor and Mrs Lewis were due to leave on *Endurance* for a visit to the Antarctic, leaving John in charge as Deputy Governor for the last few weeks of his tour. However, *Endurance*'s unfortunate argument with an uncharted rock necessitated a change of plan and we saw them off instead on *Bransfield*. This helped me in my task as with no entertaining at Government House there were not so many distractions.

The scheduled twice-monthly Albatross flights began in January and it was pleasant to have regular mail and newspapers, though it involved John in the additional chore of personally running a travel agency and conducting a furious correspondence about the need for an Elsan to be installed in the aircraft. On the Falkland Islands delegation's return flight from Buenos Aires in August, Dick Goss, who had used the convenience *en route*, made some remark to John about the tube, reminding him that an Air Force plane was for men only. Obviously, something had to be done about that before they carried children and female passengers.

With *Darwin* no longer sailing to Monte, there was a dearth of fresh fruit and the usual garden crop of gooseberries, strawberries and raspberries, to which one looked forward so eagerly at this time of year, was a dismal failure. Slugs ate the strawberries, the wind played havoc with the raspberries and the frost put paid to the gooseberries, which remained like bullets, a contrast to previous years when we invited people in to help themselves. Instead, we made do with more experts, who arrived by air. Another agronomist had already visited us; a BBC engineer now followed and then came an expert in water engineering, whose main task was to examine the efficacy of the filtration plant for the Stanley water supply, which was 15 years old. The quality of our bath water improved enormously with the right mixture of chemicals, although we continued to drink Salus.

The *Darwin* fiasco followed. The last sailing had been scheduled for the end of the year, after which she was to be withdrawn from service. A plan had been afoot for some time to sell her to the Chilean government, who seemed interested, and a date remained to be fixed for her to sail over to Punta Arenas to be inspected, at the same time enabling her to stock up with fuel. For some weeks an on–off performance followed with the Gleadell family, who were leaving the colony, putting their curtains up and down like yo-yos.

The ship eventually sailed half empty with a few round-trip passengers, but returned without any firm sale arrangements made and without having replenished its fuel tanks. *Darwin*, awkward to the last, was now very low on fuel and camp trips had to be curtailed to conserve what was left. Eventually, she had to shut down completely at the East Jetty while the crew was sent ashore until the ship's future was decided at 120 Pall Mall.

In the meantime, several visitors to the colony, including the Pettingills, a visiting ornithologist and his wife, who is the author of the book *Penguin Summer*, with lecture engagements in the States to fulfil, were becoming apprehensive about being marooned indefinitely in Stanley, while parents were becoming anxious about the schoolchildren's return to Montevideo. It was an anxious period and rumour as usual was rife. It was impossible to fit any of these people in on Albatross flights, which were already fully booked for months ahead.

Arrangements were made to fly in an extra Albatross to relieve pressure by lifting out the first scholarship children to schools in Buenos Aires, as well as two medical cases. *Endurance* put in a bid to lift out the other girls and boys, but at the last minute the plan fell through, no doubt to the disappointment of the crew. The company was unable to sail the *Darwin* to Monte as the agents there had folded up. Besides, she did not have enough fuel left to reach Monte and indeed barely enough to get anywhere except to the nearest port in Chile or Argentina.

After much discussion, planning and sending of telegrams, a compromise price was reached between the Falkland Islands Company and the Falkland Islands government for chartering *Darwin* and the ship sailed for Comodoro Rivadavia with a full passenger list, making a clear profit for the government, the week before we left the colony. An embassy official met the schoolchildren who sailed in her and accompanied them to Buenos Aires by air, where Colonel Balcarce and his wife took over to see them through immigration formalities on to the plane to Monte.

Falkland Islands Company personnel going on leave, the Pettingills and their equipment with Maurice Rumboll, the Argentine member of their team, were also able to leave by air for Buenos Aires the day after docking. Everyone in the colony heaved a sigh of relief, particularly the parents of schoolchildren who had by then long outstayed their welcome. I understand that *Darwin* is still swinging at anchor in Stanley harbour to rust away, a fate she hardly deserves.*

The Argentine Air Force wizard of engineering Mayor Remorino had again returned to Stanley, accompanied by a

* The *Darwin* left Stanley in September 1973 to continue her island hopping career in the Aegean under the name of *Crisstos K.*

civilian engineer and a surveyor attached to the Argentine Air Force, to make a more detailed assessment of the site for the temporary airstrip at Hooker's Point, not far from the main airfield site at Cape Pembroke, while, a commander of the Argentine navy had come to assess the prospects for beaching his landing craft when bringing in supplies, vehicles and machinery needed for building the airstrip.

We were also visited by a LADE representative. We showed him round town and discussed conditions and his future plans for an office and house in Stanley. This particular candidate for the assignment of LADE agent withdrew. I could see that the Falklands would naturally not be a popular posting with Argentine wives far from the sophisticated atmosphere of Buenos Aires. The choice fell finally on Mayor de la Colina, an excellent choice, as we were able to confirm when we later met him in Buenos Aires shortly before he left for Stanley with his attractive wife, whom I was able to brief on what to expect.

We were also treated to a visit by Brigadier-General Cochella of the Argentina air force. He had come to see for himself the conditions in which his agent would be working, to gain first-hand experience in flying and weather conditions on the route, and to establish personal relations with the Colony Government. He did indeed gain first-hand experience. Two aircraft made the flight from Comodoro Rivadavia on this occasion; the plane left early in good flying conditions at both ends of the route, to find on arrival at Stanley a thick blanket of cloud down to 200 feet, which refused to lift. We listened to the drone of the engines as the planes circled overhead for an hour, by which time, with the point of no return almost reached, they were obliged to fly back to the mainland. After a round trip of ten hours that day passengers and the same air crew had to be up again at 5.00 a.m. the next morning. This time the weather was kinder and they landed in Stanley harbour at approximately 10.30 a.m.

We met Brigadier-General Cochella at the air service jetty, looking quite fresh after his marathon journey, to show him round Stanley and the temporary office accommodation arranged by the government for LADE. By this time we were down to our throw-out crockery and unexpectedly faced with entertaining a General to a snack lunch. He was a charming guest who did not bat an eyelid at being presented with coffee in a mug at 11.00 a.m. and two hours later sandwiches and soup out of the same mug.

The role played by the Argentine Air Force, and in particular the aircrews of the Albatross amphibian service, cannot be underestimated. The service began officially in January 1972 and was to continue twice monthly, despite dreadful weather conditions, until the temporary airstrip opened in November of that year. Their achievement in keeping this schedule going was remarkable. The crew throughout did a marvellous public relations job of breaking the ice by establishing friendly contact with the islanders. The mercy flight had done a great deal to alleviate suspicion and the untiring efforts of the Argentine air force helped to complete the relaxation of tension. Like servicemen everywhere, collecting friends and packages on each trip, they were soon accepted by the local population.

Scenes in the cramped confined space of the airline's office at the end of the government jetty will be forever indelibly printed on my memory – the crew in their grey working uniforms with squadron flashes and Albatross emblems crowding into the small room to join Jim Kerr and Ian Campbell, the two Beaver pilots, with that easy camaraderie that always exists with flying men regardless of race – Danny Borland the 'prognosticator' leaning over the counter to demonstrate isobars and airstreams from his charts – Miriam Booth with headphones attached nursing the R/T set – more crew members arriving laden with toys from the Falkland Islands Company for their children and English cigarettes – mail bags being delivered and weighed – the fire tender standing by and the launch crew trailing the inflated baffle, which the aircrew nicknamed 'El hot dog' which acted as a buffer between launch and aircraft – Henry Luxton the Customs Officer and Harbour Master, smart in his gold braided uniform and John Jones, Colonial Secretary, keeping an overall eye on developments. Something akin to a wartime atmosphere of gaiety, daring and improvisation prevailed.

Farewells took place on the jetty from where the crew and outgoing passengers left by launch to the Albatross, lying off 100 yards or so, on the choppy water, tied to a bright scarlet buoy. Although All-Stanley soon tired of the spectacle, we never ceased to enjoy the thrill of watching the planes take off, laboured and ungainly until airborne like the bird after which they are named, slowly accelerating along the length of the harbour in a cloud of spray, rockets assisting the blast-off and the inner harbour busy with launches in attendance and a Beaver waiting to take off over the hills.

The attitude of Falkland Islanders in the face of such friendliness became one of amiable tolerance. With the twice-monthly service bringing regular mail and the fear of a medical emergency reduced, the Albatross and its crew soon became part of the local scene.

Finally, LADE the branch of the Argentine air force responsible for opening up underdeveloped regions in Argentina such as Patagonia, where conditions are similar to those in the Falkland Islands, had a vital role to play. LADE was considered ideally suited for the operation of undertaking to build and man a temporary airstrip until the British installed a permanent one. A LADE office was installed in Stanley to attend to sales and business connected with flights. Despite the difficulties of transporting equipment, supplies and machinery, and setbacks due to boggy terrain and the customary inclement weather, the Argentine team of 27 air force men, two from the army, four civil engineers and ten local workmen, all under the direction of Mayor Remorino, met the deadline. They are to be congratulated on a greal achievement.

The official opening of the temporary airstrip, celebrated with a parade, was carried out on the 15 November 1972. The Argentine air force hosted a party given in St Mary's annexe in Stanley. Fittingly, two Albatross planes had brought in the air crews who had flown the route. Equally fittingly, the Governor, on behalf of the islanders, presented them with a scroll for their services. From now on, appropriately, the route would be flown by the 'Friendship'.

Chapter 18

Partir c'est Mourir un Peu

Two days before we left the colony a farewell cocktail party was given in our honour at Government House. The Governor was kind enough to give us the choice of that or a dinner party; we chose a cocktail party as it meant that three times the number of people could he invited. As we said our farewells I had a distinct feeling of *déjà vu*, as if I had just come in!

On 28 March, on a cold, fitfully sunny but reasonably calm morning, the temperature according to Danny 8°C, I watched from the conservatory as the Albatross landed on schedule. John phoned me from his office to say that takeoff would be on time at 12.30 p.m. Our cases, carefully weighed, were already at the airline's office. In view of weight restrictions we had taken the precaution of sending advance luggage out by previous flights, to be stored for us in Buenos Aires. As we were doing an extensive journey through South America, sailing from Chile by Italian line, the one suitcase and grip permitted on Albatross flights was a bit limiting. I later was amused to see one of my cases featuring in a photograph illustrating an article in a *Daily Telegraph* colour supplement.

We had decided to stay in Sulivan House up to the last minute, which I was able to do by borrowing certain

16. My husband, J. A. Jones, OBE, Colonial Secretary and at that time Acting Governor, taking the salute, Falklands Islands, 1969–72.

essentials adding them to my stockpile of throw-out items. Mr and Mrs Heathman agreed to come in after we left to do a final cleanup and so we walked out of our Falkland Islands home after a last snack in the kitchen, leaving at midday to drive to the jetty in the PWD Mini Clubman. With a lump in my throat I left the snack practically untouched, stoked the Rayburn and shut down the dampers for the last time, and went out through the back door past the peat shed. John drove through Stanley, up and down several of the streets to take a farewell look round at the familiar scene before driving to the Government jetty where a crowd of well-wishers had gathered to see us off.

Although Lynda and Audrey, the two young women who were also leaving, laden with handbags, were clad for arrival in South America, the garb for me was, as usual, slacks and jumpers under a warm coat, as the Albatross, after lying on water for several hours, is very cold and does not begin to warm up for quite a time despite the cabin heating.

Having said our last farewells to the Governor and his wife, members of the Executive and Legislative Councils, heads of department and Stan and his wife, we clambered into *Seaspray*, Ian Campbell's launch, to be taken out by him to where Major Alvarez, the squadron commander, was readying the plane.

We waited in the launch, sheltering as best we could from the wind and spray, while the baffle was fixed against the side of the plane to prevent the launch hanging against it. Passengers were eventually invited to clamber along the rubber 'hot dog' and into the cabin, which was festooned with air/sea rescue equipment, flares, torches, R/T flex, the luggage stashed amidships and with the two rear hatches open to enable the crewman to affix the JATO rockets. Seating was arranged with due regard to the centre of gravity, with the two girls up front and ourselves amid ships, me on the port side, John on the starboard side and a visiting representative of the Argentine state Frigorífico Combine behind me. Members of the crew helped us to put on our Mae Wests which had to be worn throughout the journey and we strapped ourselves into the stark bucket seats.

We taxied down the harbour and turned into wind opposite the Upland Goose. Knowing that the takeoff would be very noisy I stuffed my ears with cotton wool, but I was unprepared for the deafening noise which continued throughout the flight making normal conversation impossible. Very slowly we began to gather speed on the run up the harbour towards the Head of the Bay. I had watched the same thing so often from Sulivan House that I recognised each phase of its progression, the roar as the amphibian strained to get up on the step, the clouds of spray obscuring the ports before the final rocket blast, but 1 was surprised to see the crewman dashing from one open hatch to the other, checking that the rockets were performing correctly. As we lifted off I looked out, blinking away the tears as we roared past Sulivan House, over the Two Sisters, across the islands and out to sea.

A hundred miles out from the Argentine coast another link was snapped as we flew over the *AES* on her way to Stanley. As we made our landfall at Comodoro Rivadavia, turning in over the harbour to land at the Air Force base, the last link was broken with the sight of *Darwin* steaming slowly southwards on her last journey back to the islands.

Epilogue

We knew of course that our links with the islands were so strongly forged as to be indissoluble. Three years there at the centre of an extremely human problem had made this inevitable and we had become part of it. So it was that immediately on reaching Comodoro Rivadavia we found ourselves dealing with matters concerning the transit of islands passengers through the port and airport, and once in Buenos Aires John was involved in tying up loose ends at the British embassy, while both of us visited islands schoolchildren experiencing their first taste of education at Anglo–Argentine schools in the capital. We had continuing public relations work to do with the British community and officials of the Argentine government and armed services.

It would in many ways have been interesting to return to the colony, but with the stimulant of 'the problem' reduced, like guests at a good party it was wise to know the psychological moment to leave. As we flew over the Cordillera of the Andes from Mendoza to Santiago on our final departure from Argentina I reflected that although the peat sods may never turn to bricks of gold our Falkland experience was a treasure trove of memories to be shared, most of all with the Kelpers who had so uniquely contributed to it.

Appendix: Joint Statement of Buenos Aires, 1 July 1971

Joint statement on communications

Special conversations were continued in Buenos Aires from 21 until 30 June 1971 about communications and movement between the Argentine mainland and the Falkland Islands by delegations of the government of the United Kingdom of Great Britain and Northern Ireland and of the Argentine republic, the former including participants from the islands. The conversations were within the general framework of the negotiations recommended by Resolution No. 2065 (XX) of the General Assembly of the United Nations and in accordance with letters addressed to the secretary-general of the organisation by the permanent representatives of both countries on 21 November 1969 and 11 December 1970. The delegates concluded that, subject to the approval of their governments, the following measures should be adopted on the understanding that they may contribute to the process of a definitive solution to the dispute between the two governments over the island which is referred to in Resolution No. 2065 (XX) mentioned above.

1. In order to deal with questions that might arise over the setting up and promotion of communications between the Argentine mainland and the Falkland Islands in both directions including questions relating to the movement

of persons, those which might arise for residents of the islands while they were on the mainland and those concerning residents of the mainland while they were in the islands, a special consultative committee should be set up, consisting of representatives of the Argentine ministry of foreign affairs and the British embassy, with its headquarters in Buenos Aires. The committee should have its representatives in Port Stanley who would keep it informed.

2. The Argentine government should issue a document, in the form annexed (description attached) to residents of the Falkland Islands irrespective of their nationality who wished to travel to the Argentine mainland, which would allow them free movement within it. A document in the same form issued by the Argentine government should be the only document needed by residents of the Argentine mainland for journeys to the Falkland Islands.

3. Residents in the Falkland Islands should be exempted by the Argentine government from all duties, taxes, and any other obligations arising as a result of activities in the Falkland Islands. In addition, residents of the Falkland Islands who go to the Argentine mainland in order to provide services connected with communications should be exempt from taxes on their salaries and other emolument which they receive from their British employers. The British government should make no claim on residents of the Argentine mainland who provide services in the Falkland Islands for activities related to communications for taxes on their salaries and other emoluments which they receive from their Argentine employers.

4. The Argentine government should take the necessary practical measures so that the normal luggage of residents of the Falkland Islands who travel between the Falkland Islands and the Argentine mainland in either direction should be free from the payment of all duties and taxes. Residents of the Falkland Islands should be exempted from the payment of all Argentine duties and taxes in respect of their luggage, household effects and motorcars passing directly through the Argentine mainland towards the Falkland Islands or going abroad through the Argentine mainland. The British government should take the necessary measures so that the normal luggage of residents of the Argentine mainland who travel between the Argentine mainland and the Falkland Islands in either direction will be exempted from the payment of all duties and taxes.

5. The Argentine government should take the necessary measures so that each resident of the island who establishes a permanent residence on the Argentine mainland may bring in once only free of all duties and taxes all personal effects, household effects and a motorcar. Equally, the British government should take the necessary measures so that each resident on the Argentine mainland who establishes a permanent residence in the Falkland Islands, may bring in once only free of all duties and taxes all personal effects, household effects and a motorcar.

6. The British and Argentine governments should facilitate in the Falkland Islands and on the Argentine mainland respectively, the transit, residence and work of persons directly concerned with practical measure adopted in

order to implement and promote communications and movement.

7. The British government should take the necessary measures to arrange for a regular shipping service for passengers, cargo and mail between the Falkland Islands and the Argentine mainland.

8. The Argentine government should take the necessary measures to arrange for a regular service of weekly frequency by air for passengers, cargo and mail between the Argentine mainland and the Falkland Islands.

9. Pending the completion of the airfield at Port Stanley, the Argentine government should provide a temporary service by amphibian aircraft between the Argentine mainland and the Falkland Islands for passengers' cargo and mail. This service should be reviewed from time to time in the light of progress in the construction of the airfield mentioned above.

10. Both governments should cooperate over the simplifycations of administrative practices, regulations and documentation for sea and air transport bearing in mind the need to promote and speed up comniunication.

11. In order to facilitate the movement of persons born in the Falkland Islands the Argentine government should take the necessary measures to exempt them from all obligations for enlistment and military service. The British government should declare that in the Falkland Islands no obligations for enlistment for military service exist.

12. Both governments should study and exchange views on measures to facilitate trade and to permit a greater case of commercial transaction.

13. The British and Argentine governments should take the necessary measures so that postal, telegraphic and telephone communications in both directions between the Argentine mainland and the Falkland Islands are as effective and expeditious as possible.

14. The tariff for postal, telegraphic and telephone communications in the directions between the Argentine mainland and the Falkland Islands should be at a rate equivalent to the internal rate at the place or origin of the communications.

15. Postage stamps on mail travelling between the Argentine mainland and Falkland Islands in either direction should be cancelled with a mark referring to this joint statement. Mail bags should he similarly marked.

16. The Argentine government should be prepared to cooperate in the health, educational, agricultural and technical fields if so requested. The Argentine government should arrange for places to be available in schools on the Argentine mainland for the children of residents of the Falkland Islands and should offer scholarships that should he published from time to time, the number of which should be decided upon in the light of local requirements. Both governments should continue to exchange views on the matters referred to in this paragraph.

17. Conversations should he continued through the customary diplomatic channels and the next meeting should he held in Port Stanley in 1972.

18. If either government should decide to terminate the measures referred to above, it should give six months' notice of its decision to the other government.

Initialled in Buenos Aires on the 1st day of July 1971 by the heads of the respective delegations.

Index